MORE PRAISE FOR *WELL NOURISHED*

"This book is medicine for your soul. It will take you on a journey exploring the different aspects of your self, showing you how to receive deep nourishment and be happy from the inside out. The clear, powerful practices give you tangible ways to balance and nourish your own life and, through your own fulfilled life, help nourish the world."

—Marci Shimoff, *New York Times* best-selling author of *Happy for No Reason*

"*Well Nourished* is a beautiful book. Its message is not about depriving ourselves of food but truly serving ourselves with a feast that supports health, happiness, and a meaningful life. I highly recommend this wise and loving book that guides us in living the life we want to be living."

—Bob Stahl, Ph.D., co-author of *A Mindfulness-Based Stress Reduction Workbook, Living With Your Heart Wide Open, Calming the Rush of Panic, A Mindfulness-Based Stress Reduction Workbook for Anxiety,* and *MBSR Everyday*

"The spirit of this book is all encompassing, creating a path to higher wisdom through deepening our relationship to food, eating, and our bodies. This broad wisdom is complemented by many practical elements to help you along the way; tools to be used and questions to be reflected on, drawing on that capacity for mindfulness that we all have to cultivate deeper understanding and balance."

—Jean L. Kristeller, Ph.D., author of *The Joy of Half a Cookie*

"*Well Nourished* is a rich and comprehensive guidebook that not only helps the reader establish a healthy relationship to food, but also uses it as a vehicle to greater experience consciousness, mindfulness, and true fulfillment in all areas of one's life. As a result, it allows your goodness to shine through and help awaken it in those around you. An excellent offering."

—James Baraz, author of *Awakening Joy: 10 Steps to Happiness* and co-founding teacher, Spirit Rock Meditation Center, Woodacre, California

"Andrea Lieberstein's *Well Nourished* is a delightful feast combining behavioral science research, practical exercises, and a heathy dose of personal and professional experience. She has crafted a sensible and compassionate guide to nourishing yourself in body, mind, and spirit."

—David S. Sobel, M.D., M.P.H., former medical director of Patient Education for Kaiser Permanente Northern California and author of *Healthy Pleasures*

Inspiring | Educating | Creating | Entertaining

Brimming with creative inspiration, how-to projects, and useful information to enrich your everyday life, Quarto Knows is a favorite destination for those pursuing their interests and passions. Visit our site and dig deeper with our books into your area of interest: Quarto Creates, Quarto Cooks, Quarto Homes, Quarto Lives, Quarto Drives, Quarto Explores, Quarto Gifts, or Quarto Kids.

First Published in 2017 by Fair Winds Press, an imprint of The Quarto Group, 100 Cummings Center, Suite 265-D, Beverly, MA 01915, USA.
T (978) 282-9590 F (978) 283-2742 QuartoKnows.com

Fair Winds Press titles are also available at discount for retail, wholesale, promotional, and bulk purchase. For details, contact the Special Sales Manager by email at specialsales@quarto.com or by mail at The Quarto Group, Attn: Special Sales Manager, 401 Second Avenue North, Suite 310, Minneapolis, MN 55401, USA.

21 20 19 18 17   1 2 3 4 5

ISBN: 978-1-59233-752-1
Digital edition published in 2017

Library of Congress Cataloging-in-Publication Data available

Design and page layout: Laura McFadden Design, Inc.
Cover Image: Glenn Scott Photography
Illustration: Mattie Wells

Printed in China

The information in this book is for educational purposes only. It is not intended to replace the advice of a physician or medical practitioner. Please see your health-care provider before beginning any new health program. If you suspect you may have an eating disorder, please seek professional help to support you on the journey. A team approach is very helpful, including a registered dietitian nutritionist, psychotherapist, and physician.

WELL NOURISHED

Mindful Practices to Heal Your Relationship with Food, Feed Your Whole Self, and End Overeating

Andrea Lieberstein M.P.H., R.D.N.

FAIR WINDS

DEDICATION

*To David and Joshua for your love, support, and joy
on our journey together*

*May my words, thoughts, and actions today contribute to the happiness,
freedom, and peace of all beings. May all be happy, may all be peaceful, may all be
free, may no one know suffering on my account or that of any others.*
~A LOVINGKINDNESS WISH FOR ALL BEINGS

Contents

INTRODUCTION

Well Nourished is a whole-person, non-diet approach to mindful eating and living that has evolved from my more than twenty-five years working with clients to improve lives through mindful care. It offers a guide to whole-body nourishment where you can throw away the food rules, learn to listen to your total-body wisdom, yet still utilize the support of sound nutrition and health knowledge.

It's easy to focus on diets and eating as the answer to all of our problems, but this can come at the expense of paying attention to the other areas of our lives. Of course, balanced eating and exercise are foundational for good health, but unless we nourish all the parts of ourselves, our lives can feel empty at the core, devoid of meaning and fulfillment. No matter how much we work on our diet and exercise programs, we cannot fill this void without addressing the emotional, spiritual, creative, social, and psychological nourishment we really crave. None of the parts of ourselves exists in a vacuum. For true change to occur we need to understand how tending to each part touches, uplifts, and strengthens all the other parts. We can create a healthy, vibrant web of life in our own bodies that extends out to others through our positive actions, thoughts, deeds, and love.

Being "well nourished" goes beyond food. By discerning what you are truly hungry for, you can feed the other parts of yourself as needed and be supported in making choices that best nurture your total well-being—mind, body, heart, and spirit. This book introduces the core basics you need to get started. Mindfulness is a unifying factor that will help you tune in to your body, mind, and heart and figure out what each really needs at any particular moment. The mini-assessments and explanations about how our mind and body work give you the groundwork to evaluate what is sensible for you, and the mindful tools and practices let you put your plan into action.

Mindfulness can powerfully heal your relationship to food (and really almost any area you are struggling with), particularly when applied to all aspects of your life. When you see clearly who you really are, and the gifts that ensue, your perspective may be restored. The focus on and struggle with food can become less overwhelming when you nurture other parts of your life. With more balance, you can enjoy and savor your entire life fully. Mindful eating and living as approached in *Well Nourished* is a wonderful way to heal your relationship not only with food but also with your body, your heart, your mind, and your life.

How to Use This Book

I hope you will read this book with the spirit of an explorer, an adventurer, a scientist—with an open mind and kind, nonjudgmental attention. Change begins one step at a time. You have your own unique palette of your life with which to paint. Do it in a way that comes from your deepest self and have some fun while doing it too.

There is a lot of information here, and many useful steps and practices that may be new for you. So you can approach this book in any way that works. You could:

1.   Work through each chapter at your own pace, applying the 5 steps as you go in the real time of your life.

2.   Read through the chapters in order, taking the mini-assessments as you work through the awareness stage and setting intentions, then go back and apply all 5 steps to the areas you decide you want to focus on, whether those that are the most undernourished or simply the parts you are drawn to. Chapter 3 has a process to help you prioritize if you choose this approach.

3.   Simply read through the book, deciding when you want to come back and actually work through the 5 steps in each chapter.

If you are reading and working through the book systematically, chapter by chapter, you will need to prioritize areas of focus along the way. You might choose small goals for each chapter; you might focus on the areas where you have the most energy and interest; or you might decide to go deeply into one area that has many different components, like physical nourishment (which includes mindful eating, nutrition, sleep, exercise, and more).

Part 1 offers a framework for nourishing your whole self, coming back into balance, healing your relationship to food, and potentially helping with other struggles. If we are out of balance in any area of our lives, we may turn to food to feed our need for nourishment and desire for pleasure. This can be a problem when we overeat, leading to cycles of distress and imbalance. We may find we are no longer enjoying our food. The foundational mindful eating practices that you'll learn here will help you begin to recalibrate your relationship with food to that of true nourishment and pleasure in the right quantity for you.

In part 2 you'll be introduced to the 5 steps to mindful eating and living and you'll visit in more depth each of the core "bodies" that make up our whole self. The idea that we are comprised of different bodies is found in other traditions in the world, such as the five koshas in yogic philosophy. We recognize that, across cultures, these bodies are universal parts of ourselves and what make us uniquely human. You'll begin these chapters with a personal assessment of the different aspects of lifestyle that contribute to well-being, nourishment, and balance. You'll see that when each one of these areas is nourished according to your personal needs, they can support eating mindfully and having a healthy relationship to food. With tools, practices, and a plan, you'll be guided to bring these areas into balance to support mindful eating and living.

Self-kindness will be a great companion on this journey and one we will revisit again and again. As with anything in life, the more you put into the program, the more benefits you will receive. It takes time to unravel the habits you have cultivated over time. I look forward to guiding you on this journey to crafting a fulfilling, well-nourished life. Enjoy!

PART
1

Essential Ingredients for a Well~Nourished Life

CHAPTER ONE

Nourishing the Whole Self: What Are You Truly Hungry For?

When our mind, body, and spirit are fully nourished, we can enjoy and savor food for its own sake. We no longer need to rely on food to substitute for other sources of nourishment.

Nourishment comes from many sources. Many people use food to nourish themselves when what they are really hungry for is another form of fulfillment. They are looking to fill empty spaces in their lives rather than their stomachs. What if you were living a life where you felt well nourished on all levels—emotionally, intellectually, physically, psychologically, spiritually, socially, and creatively? This book explores how, through mindful eating and living, you can best nourish yourself on all levels. When your body, mind, and spirit are fully nourished, you can enjoy and savor food for its own sake without relying on it for other needs. You are able to come into mindful balance with food and living.

You may have picked up this book because you want to feel better. You want to get your eating under control, lose weight, and be healthier. You know there is more to living than what you have been experiencing. You want to feel better nourished in all aspects of your day-to-day life and you know that you can't keep depending on food to be your primary source of fulfillment. You may simply want a more mindful relationship to food and to be in better balance with the different parts of your life. You've come to the right place. In this book, we explore how to craft a well-nourished life with a plan that can be individualized to you and your unique needs.

Mindful Expectations

The key tool we will come back to again and again is mindfulness. Mindfulness is a way of learning to pay attention in the moment to your inner experiences, including thoughts, feelings, impulses, and cravings. It is a way to acknowledge and meet your inner and outer experiences with patience, kindness, and nonjudgment. When you live this way, you are better able to see clearly and make wise choices. When you utilize mindful awareness to recognize that life is change, you can navigate it more skillfully without getting bent out of shape when the day, the week, or the moment doesn't go your way.

No matter how much we plan or schedule a routine to incorporate healthy lifestyle habits and practice good stress management and mindfulness, life just happens. Unexpected events, inconveniences, or demands can throw us a curveball. This can be frustrating even if we know that change is a natural part of life. Not just the big things can get to us, like moving, changing jobs, or going through a separation, but also the day-to-day, moment-to-moment changes: The cat gets sick, the car breaks down, a trip to the bank takes much longer than expected, a work meeting runs late, the school calls to say your child has become ill, ouch, the list goes on. It is natural and part of being human to constantly adjust our lives to restore balance. We tend to juggle many balls and at the same time have different parts of us that need care, attention, and nurturing.

The frustration with the day or week not meeting expectations might lead to habitual cravings at different times of the day that manifest as various hungers. It may seem as if fulfilling the cravings will make you feel better, but the fix is only temporary. Many people, including some of my clients, use food to numb themselves, zone out, and find comfort, while others rely on television, alcohol, or other substances. Some overwork or keep themselves excessively busy with errands, projects, and accomplishments. These may all lead to an immediate sense of gratification but do not fill the void or address the sense of fatigue, emptiness, unsettledness, unease, or lack of fulfillment in the moment or in the daily routine.

People often eat for reasons that have nothing to do with true physical hunger. Food can be an easy way to soothe and fill. But at what cost? You are likely consuming calories that you don't really need. You are probably eating the food mindlessly, unaware of the taste, the pleasure and satisfaction that could be available if you were fully present. You may have accompanying feelings of guilt, shame, or stress around eating mindlessly. These recurring feelings might even carry over to other times of the day when you are truly hungry and taint the simple act of eating a meal. However subtle, they can rob you of the full experience of eating as a source of joy, pleasure, and well-being.

What if you could discern what you were *really* needing in that moment? What if you could give it to yourself, or, if it wasn't available, make a conscious choice—be it to eat or not—that you can feel good about? Perhaps you really needed a nap or rest in the middle of a workday (which may not have been possible) but you ate a bag of potato chips or a candy bar instead. In the moment it may have felt good, but as it settles in your stomach you feel bloated, overly full, and are now judging yourself. With the approach in this book you will be able to see more options and make mindful choices and lifestyle adjustments in just such moments. You will learn to assess why you were so tired in the first place and find a healthy, nonfood way to rejuvenate and energize yourself—or make a mindful food choice that will support your health and energy levels. You can meet each moment fresh, without expectations, and make decisions that best serve you and that meet your intentions. You will notice when you are on automatic pilot—then intentionally come back to the moment and see what you actually need.

By stepping back and assessing your life, and the cycle of your days and habits, you'll be able to identify where you may be lacking nourishment, be malnourished, or even be undernourished. By discerning what you are truly hungry for, you can learn to integrate practices and tools that will keep you nourished—inside and out.

Nourishing the Eight Bodies

To begin this journey, we are going to look at the different aspects of our lives that make us uniquely human. Obviously our physical body needs food, water, rest, and exercise; in addition, we have other "bodies" that need to be cared for in order for us to feel fulfilled. All these aspects of ourselves need nourishment and attention just as our physical body does.

These different bodies are interrelated and affected by each other, particularly by the physical body. For example, if you aren't taking care of your physical body, then you may not feel like being creative or you may find it hard to focus on intellectual activities. Let's take a look more closely at each of these "bodies" and the important role they play in feeding our whole self. Some may be more important to you than others to develop or nourish. Bringing awareness to the areas in our life where we are lacking is the first step to sustainable change.

Physical Body

Our physical body needs the proper balance of food, water, sleep, exercise, movement, and rest and relaxation in order to thrive. If one or more of these components are missing or lacking, we may have a general feeling of malaise, stress, unease, fatigue, tension, anxiety, or depression. We might try to overcome these feelings by eating more than our body requires or eating the kinds of highly processed foods that are full of sugar, fat, salt, and/or refined carbohydrates—common go-to foods when things are out of balance. Or we might overwork or drink too much to try to feel better.

Let's look at a more specific example: It has been a week since you last went to the gym, walked briskly for half an hour or so, or took your regular yoga class. You have a lot going on with work, managing your kids' after-school activities and homework, as well as dealing with household chores like cooking, cleaning, and laundry. You've postponed your nourishing social engagements and feel a general buildup of tension in your body. The refrigerator has your name on it and has become your friend after dinner. But eating doesn't fix the problem. Self-judging thoughts and guilt can immediately follow as well as feeling physically uncomfortably full. Nourishing the body through exercise, which increases feelings of well-being and discharges tension, could have been helpful here, as could have keeping a few social engagements that were fun, supportive, or stress-relieving.

Keeping your physical body well nourished establishes a foundation of wellness and well-being that can help you stay balanced in your eating and lifestyle habits and impacts all the other bodies. It helps you to receive and give nourishment in all aspects of your life. Exercise is just one example of physical nourishment that can affect the way we eat and live. Diet, of course, is another. We will visit the role of social nourishment shortly, which can actually impact physical health as well.

Emotional Body

How would you describe your general emotional tone? Do your moods swing up and down, or do you tend to be steady or have particular emotions that predominate? How do you typically feel when you are under stress? Some people experience anxiety, others depression or anger. We all have our predispositions and individual temperaments. When we are well nourished and have many resources, we tend to be more even and experience more positive emotion. We can draw on these resources when we are under stress and thus find equilibrium more quickly. One such resource to nourish our emotional body is mindfulness. Mindfulness can not only help us manage difficult emotions and situations with a sense of peace and control but also help us cultivate more of the pleasant emotions and positive qualities of mind, such as kindness, appreciation, gratitude, and joy. Cultivating nourishment in all the bodies will support our emotional body as well.

Let's say you had a hard day at work. Nothing seemed to go right. You skipped lunch because of a deadline. When you got home, you were so tired from the stress of the day and not eating enough that you skipped your evening walk as well. You made a healthy dinner but snacked during the preparation because you were so hungry you couldn't wait. You ate more overall than you wanted to and weren't happy about that. Dinner is over, and now you are feeling sad and lonely. You have your eye on the cupcakes you bought for the work potluck tomorrow.

How could you nourish the emotional body in that moment? You might automatically go for the cupcakes. Or you might decide to nourish your heart. Chapter 5 is full of practices that can help. Just a few examples might be engaging in a mindful, heart-centered practice where you become your own compassionate best friend, calling a buddy, cuddling with your cat or partner, or engaging in a creative or intellectual pursuit to help nourish the emotional body. It may be that in this instance, a need to feel love and connection with yourself or others after a challenging day is behind the desire for the cupcakes. You also may notice that attending to the physical body that evening or earlier in the day by doing some gentle stretching or walking or eating a good lunch may have helped your emotional body later on.

Psychological Body

Our psychological body includes not only our thoughts but our feelings as well as our awareness. Since there is an overlap here with the other bodies, we will explore this area particularly as it pertains to the realm of mindfulness and being present in our moment-to-moment experience with kindness, compassion, and nonjudgment. We will consider our relationship to what is happening in our thoughts, feelings, and awareness. Are you on automatic pilot, habitually going through your days without attention or care to the nourishment of your different bodies except to get the next deadline, errand, or project done? Do you approach yourself and your experiences with kindness and compassion, or do you tend to judge yourself frequently?

In the example of the day where you are eyeing the cupcakes, you might decide to eat the cupcakes without much thought to what else you may really need in the moment. After eating one cupcake, the judging mind might set in: "Why did I eat that cupcake? I wanted to lose weight. I'm a bad person with no willpower. I've ruined my diet today, so I may as well eat more." And you end up eating the whole package.

With mindful awareness, you might pause before or after eating one cupcake and notice how tired you are, and that the loneliness you are experiencing is a result of feeling disconnected from yourself after a hard day with little rest or other nourishment. You notice you aren't hungry anymore and feel overfull from dinner and all the pre-dinner snacking. What might truly nourish you in this moment rather than eating the cupcakes? How might bringing kindness to the thoughts that are beating you up stop the cycle of mindlessly eating? You may then choose to nourish yourself after your long day with a bubble bath, a heart-based practice, or curling up with your favorite book or movie.

What if you had a toolbox of powerful mindful-eating practices that would help you savor and enjoy what you *do* choose to eat—but help you eat only the amounts that you can feel good about? Mindfulness will help you identify what you really need on an ongoing basis. Your awareness, intentions, and toolbox will help guide you and support your choices.

Social Body

Scientists can actually measure how the brain and body positively respond to social connection, a loving touch, or a great talk with a friend. This bonding relaxes us and can produce oxytocin, a "care-giving" hormone, bonding and other health benefits. But perceived barriers of time, "too many things to do," or an emotional body being out of balance (such as feeling overwhelmed and depressed) may prevent us from regularly tapping into the nourishment this important part of life can bring.

Going back to the earlier example of the challenging workday in our discussion of the physical body, we can consider how the day might have ended differently if you had made a positive social connection. Reaching for the phone to call a friend or spending quality time with a spouse or partner—rather than reaching for the cupcakes—probably would have left you feeling more fulfilled and in control of the circumstances.

Intellectual Body

The desire to learn new things is part of being human. It has helped us survive and thrive as a species. The intellect embodies our natural curiosity and quest for understanding. Some people love to learn for learning's sake or enjoy abstract or academic ideas. Some people love to read books, go to lectures, listen to music, build model cars, or take apart computers and put them back together. The intellectual body is one that is important to nourish, as it often gets left behind when we are busy and overwhelmed with day-to-day responsibilities. For some people having regular intellectual outlets and stimulation enriches the soul, like creativity, and is very fulfilling.

Perhaps underneath the craving for ice cream at 8:00 p.m. is a desire for stimulation and engagement, but food is the habit. The sweetness and creaminess of ice cream are more immediately tangible than reading the novel lying on your coffee table, watching a documentary, or going out to a theater performance with friends. Mindfulness can help you break this habit, discern which body is hungry and what would really feed your intellect. In chapter 8 you will assess how the intellectual body applies to you and what would be particularly helpful to nourish this area.

Creative Body

When we are engaged in a creative activity, we enter a state sometimes called flow, which is the opposite of the stress response. Creative pursuits can be fun, relaxing, and all-absorbing, thus taking our mind off other worries and helping us be completely present in the moment. For some people absorption in creative activities may feel like food for the soul. Depending on your personal interests, your creative outlet may be making beautiful art, cooking a gourmet meal, or writing a poem or short story. Perhaps you have completely let go of this facet of your life after you entered the workforce or had a family. Or maybe you have recently retired from a job that provided creative opportunities and now feel a dearth of creative activity in your life.

Reflecting on the example of the challenging day at work, think about how things would have ended differently if you had engaged in a creative activity that you enjoy. What if you had spent the evening playing an instrument you love or working on that novel you always promise yourself you are going to write? How might your creative activities have nourished you after an exhausting day? How might this have affected possible trips to the refrigerator that evening?

Spiritual Body

Another kind of hunger that is not always recognized is spiritual hunger. Being fed spiritually can be quite transformational, an important part of a fulfilling and balanced life.

We all have unique ways of relating with, understanding, and experiencing what is spiritual. For some the sense of being connected to something greater than ourselves is experienced by spending time in nature. For others, it is experienced during a religious ritual or service. Some feel a sense of the spiritual in community, while for others it is in solitary meditation or prayer. The details of how you experience the spiritual aren't important—only that you find the space to do so. How often do you allow yourself to contemplate the greater mystery of life or rest in a sense of great love? What lifts your soul?

Consider the earlier example of the stressful day at work. What if you were regularly reading inspirational books at bedtime or had a daily meditation or yoga practice that nourished you? What if you took a few minutes out of each day to watch the sunrise in the morning or look at the stars in the evening? Or perhaps you participated in a spiritual study group once a week or took a quiet walk in nature? Consider how cultivating a connection with a sense of something greater than yourself, however that may look for you, could be deeply nourishing and help maintain mindful eating practices and more balanced eating.

Worldly Nourishment

Feeling that you are a part of the world and making a difference in some way is another vital area of nourishment that is sometimes overlooked. When you feel you are making a meaningful contribution and have a sense of purpose in your life, it can be easier to get up in the morning. Stress and cortisol—known as the stress hormone—levels can be lower. You might notice more of a sense of energy and enthusiasm. People who have a sense of purpose are healthier in general and live longer. It seems it even helps your brain be more resilient and age better.

Everyone has his or her own unique gifts and talents. Are you aware of what yours are, and are you actively expressing them in the world? Do you feel you have a venue to share your talents and gifts through work, volunteerism, family, your community, or in some other way? Or are you using food to stuff away feelings of frustration from not manifesting this area in your life? Imagine a day where you made some meaningful contribution in work or to your family or community in some way. How did you feel afterward? How did it impact your day? You might notice it makes you feel good and mentally upbeat. You have an internal sense of well-being and energy from contributing to something you care deeply about. How might this impact your self-care choices on this day? Could it reduce stress eating? Affect the types of food you choose and their quantity? It doesn't matter how big your contribution is. One action, however small, can make a big difference in someone's life.

· ·

If you picked up this book, then something in you is ready for a change. You may have become tired of how out-of-balance your focus on food and eating is and want more tools to manage it. You know you can feel better. You are ready to lead a well-nourished, more creatively expressed life. Change is possible with small, doable steps.

The first step is shining the light of your awareness on how your life is now. We will take a closer look at each of the bodies in upcoming chapters and deeply assess what you are truly hungry for. What areas in your life are most undernourished?

Feeling whole and balanced makes a difference in our emotional state, our daily eating habits, and how we take care of ourselves. As you find balance, you will want to put more attention and energy into taking care of all of your bodies. This in turn will nourish the only physical body you will ever have in this life. Each small step you make in increasing nourishment in the areas that are important to you will feed all the other bodies as well. Eating and living mindfully reinforces itself. However, in order to successfully integrate mindful eating and living practices you first need to clarify and define your objectives around self-nourishment.

Define Your Vision and Destination

Having a clear overall intention for why you are embarking on this journey is an important key to staying motivated, and the tools and practices here can keep you on track. Below, I have offered a few common intentions that people I've worked with over the years have chosen for themselves. Notice how the list changes as you continue to read. I've offered additional suggestions to inspire you, lift your intentions up, or help you if you are feeling stuck with your own. Choose an overall vision or intention for your own life that resonates with you—or create your own.

My Overall Intention Is . . .

"I want to look better."

"I want to get my eating under control and lose weight."

"I want to feel better."

"I'd like to be healthy."

"I want to feel good in my life."

"I want to find a new, sustainable way to feel good, healthy, and balanced."

"I want to learn how to have a peaceful and nurturing relationship with food."

"I want to be happier and more at peace."

"I want to be free of all the negative self-criticism and judgments in my head and find peace and enjoy life again!"

"I want to lead a well-nourished, more creatively expressed life."

"I want to be healthier because I care deeply about myself and being there for those I love and care about in my life."

"I want to nourish my body as much as possible because I want to live a long, healthy life to_____ (e.g., be there for my family, my children, my grandchildren, to manifest my life's work and passion, to make the world a better place . . .)."

What do you notice about the qualities of these sample intentions as you go down the list? The first few are very common and are often linked to pressure felt through cultural norms and media portrayals of the perfect appearance and weight. Some amount of anxiety and preoccupation with weight and looks frequently goes along with these types of intentions. As we move down the list, the intentions become broader and linked to values that the people find important in their lives. They may feel more inspiring. We find through research that when intentions are expanded and include deeper personal values, they are more powerful motivators and are linked to longer and healthier lives! Your driving force is no longer linked to reasons that create fear and anxiety, which ultimately are not positive or successful motivators.

List Your Personal Values

What is very important to you? What do you value in your life? Perhaps it is health and wellness, family, community service, nature, fulfilling your life's work, and manifesting your unique gifts. It can also include personal values such as kindness, creativity, compassion, integrity, courage, and friendship. Record some of your values below and/or in your Well Nourished Journal (see page 23):

_____

_____

Write Your Overall Intention

Now that you've established your personal values, take some time to write out your overall intention for living a well-nourished life. If losing weight or looking good is the first thing that comes to mind, broaden it beyond the strictly physical or surface reason to how being well nourished may contribute to the personal values you've listed above. Intentions are most powerful when they are based on reasons that come from your deepest values. Access a sense of deep care and regard for yourself as you write your intention. If this feels too difficult, you can access this place by imagining the caring words a friend, parent, teacher, or benefactor would say to you. What would they be? Perhaps put a hand over your heart as you contemplate your caring intention for yourself.

Put your intention into positive language and the present moment as if it is occurring now. Alternatively it may be a positive wish of well-being for yourself. You might write a longer intention and then have a short version to remember in the moment when faced with myriad choices throughout each day. For example:

"May I make choices that support my health and well-being in each moment."
Shorter version: *"I make choices that support my health and well-being."*
"Taking care of myself is my highest priority so I may be my best self for myself and others."
Shorter version: *"Taking care of myself is my highest priority."*
"I make choices to lead a well-nourished life with kindness and compassion in each moment."
Shorter versions: *"I am making kind choices that support a well-nourished life."*
"I make choices that support and nourish me."
"I am staying in balance and living with ease as I _____ (e.g., start my dream nonprofit, head a committee at my child's school, write my book, start my new company, take care of my parents . . .)."
Shorter version: *"I am staying in balance and living with ease."*

It's important to realize that we don't have to be perfect. Taking care of yourself can include being compassionate and kind to yourself when you don't "reach the mark" or stay on track. Our choices can vary slightly day to day depending upon circumstances and conditions. You might consider adding one of these intentions or one that is similar to support your flight plan.

"I remember to be kind and compassionate to myself."
"I offer love and kindness to myself in each moment."

Write your overall intention below and/or in your Well Nourished Journal—both the long and any short version:

My overall intention is:

_____

_____

_____

Shorter version:

_____

_____

Fuel Your Journey with Your Intention

Your overall intention will be the guiding light that helps move you forward. You can use it to plan your day and to align your choices in each moment. Call upon it, remember it, pull it out as you need to. Then ask yourself what tools, practices, and information you have (or need) to make choices that are aligned with this intention.

Throughout the book, I will be asking you to record not only your intentions but also your thoughts and experiences, and to answer specific questions and complete written exercises. You will need a dedicated "Well Nourished" journal or notebook to begin this journey, or you may write directly in this book.

In the next chapter we'll explore how you can use food mindfully for nourishment. Your thoughts and beliefs impact how you eat, and mindfulness can help you navigate them with awareness so your approach to food becomes self-nourishing, not self-limiting. This will be the first stop on your journey to feeding the whole self. Then as we go throughout the book, you'll learn how to discern your true needs so you can skillfully expand the ways you care for yourself beyond physical hunger.

CHAPTER TWO

Food As Nourishment: Mindfully Transforming How You Eat

When we rest our full attention on our food, each bite can become an act of pure joy. We feel our connection to the earth, the sunshine, the rain, the goodness of nature that becomes incorporated into our body.

Many of us take food for granted, not giving it much attention. This chapter explores the how of eating, rather than the what. We'll look at attitudes, beliefs, habits, and behaviors and the ways these support or sabotage our efforts to enjoy our food, feel at peace, and eat in a nourishing and healthful manner.

Think about your relationship to food. Is the attention you put on food mostly positive, negative, or neutral? Where do you fall along the spectrum? Wherever you are, you came to this book because you wanted to make changes. Whatever you've been doing isn't fully working for you, and you are ready for an approach that involves your whole self.

How Do You Eat Now?

What changes in your eating habits and relationship to food specifically are you wishing to make? Write below and/or in your Well Nourished Journal some of those changes. For example:

~ I simply enjoy eating and would like to create more time in my life to consciously plan, purchase, prepare, and eat delicious food easefully and mindfully.

~ I am constantly losing and gaining weight, am unhappy with my weight, compare myself to others, and try the latest diet. I get confused by the conflicting information about nutrition and am tired of the yo-yoing up and down. I want to get off the seesaw and find a new, healthy, balanced relationship with food.

~ I don't struggle with my weight, but I want to learn how to eat in a way that feels satisfying and good to my body.

~ I'd like to be more mindful about portion size, especially of the highly processed salty or sweet foods. How can I make more nutritious and tasty choices for the health of my body?

What is true for you?

Balance Eating Patterns and Attention

Through learning and practicing mindfulness, and using the tools and practices in this book, you will be able to bring your eating patterns and the attention you put on food into balance with the rest of your life. You'll free up energy, time, and mental space to focus on nourishing all the parts of yourself in the particular ways that work for you. That may mean less focus on food (including food thoughts, worry, guilt, body shame) or more attention on planning for nutritious, healthy choices and all that entails. Whatever it looks like for you, learning to pay attention in a mindful way will be a key to transforming your relationship with food and bringing all the other parts of yourself and your life into equilibrium.

There are so many situations and circumstances that affect our food choices, the amounts we eat, and how much we actually enjoy these foods. In this chapter we will explore how food can nourish us—mind, body, and spirit—no matter the situation, so that we can have the health, radiance, and energy to live our lives, to love, and to pursue our dreams.

Let's take a closer look at some of your current habits and relationship with food. Take out your Well Nourished Journal, sit quietly, and reflect for a moment as you answer the following questions.

Is the way I eat now truly nourishing me?

1. Do I usually savor and enjoy my food?
2. Do I generally eat when I'm hungry and stop just before or when I am comfortably full?
3. Do I know how to eat in a way that is best for me?
4. Do I overeat on a regular basis?
5. Do I often eat to procrastinate, soothe away uncomfortable feelings, or because food is there?
6. Do I frequently eat while engaging in other activities (e.g., reading, watching TV, cooking) without paying attention to quantity, taste, or satisfaction?
7. Do I often feel spacey or sluggish after meals?
8. Do I frequently judge myself about the choices and amounts of food that I eat?
9. Do I judge the way my body looks and feels after eating?
10. Do I feel guilty about eating desserts or other foods?

Did you gain any new awareness of how your relationship to food may be affecting your experience of eating? If you answered yes to any of the questions besides the first three, then you have room to improve your relationship with food. Eating doesn't have to be a struggle with flavors of guilt or judgment lingering long after we finished our last bite. Nor are we sentenced to eating to overfull or stuffed for the rest of our lives. You can change the habits that leave you unconsciously eating through the bag of potato chips, cookies, or entire fruit bowl while engaged in some other activity. You can change the habits that leave you feeling bloated, tired, or sluggish to those that leave you feeling good, energized, vibrant, and healthy.

By paying attention to your body and the types of foods you eat and having a good understanding of basic nutrition principles you can find a way of eating that will help you thrive. Through mindful eating you can find more peace with food, enjoying it in the right quantity and quality for your body and experiencing true nourishment.

A key to balance is applying mindful attention to the entire process of eating. With mindfulness, you can polish the lens of your attention to be present for planning, preparing, choosing, and enjoying your food. We are taking eating out of the realm of automatic pilot, unconsciousness, and little or no planning to a thoughtful approach so that our minds, bodies, and spirits can be nourished by our food.

Mindful Attention

Mindfulness is a way of paying attention with kindness and without judgment. We train the mind to become present by resting on whatever activity we are doing—walking, eating, resting, writing. Our minds are usually so busy focusing on the future, thinking about the past, worrying, reminiscing. This is the nature of the mind—it wanders on its own. And we can be at the whim of it. Or we can develop the ability to simply notice when it is wandering through mindfulness practice, choose whether we want to be on that train of thought (is it helpful or additive to my experience right now?) or come back to what is true in this moment.

There is a place for planning, reminiscing, daydreaming, of course, but much of this happens without our awareness. It can take us away from being fully present to live this moment—to enjoy the food we are eating, to listen to our bodies, to really hear our loved ones. Learning to be more in the present helps us to rest in our hearts and be free of aimless buffeting from an agitated mind. We have tools to calm the mind and ease the struggle (however subtle) from resisting our experience of life in the moment, which makes for smoother sailing.

Chapter 3 introduces the foundational practice of mindfulness meditation and how it can help us cultivate this kind of attention.

Mindfulness Nourishes Our Eating

When we are calm and present with full attention on our food, we can most fully receive nourishment on the mind, body, and spirit levels. With a quiet, present mind and body we are receptive to the nuances of the eating experience, including pleasure and satisfaction. We can savor our food fully with our senses, bringing delight, joy, and other positive emotions. We can be more attuned to our hunger and satiety signals, guiding us toward when to begin or finish eating.

But many things get in the way of our receiving full nourishment from food, so we must practice making our mindfulness stronger. The thoughts in our minds, our emotional states, the environment, and our physical states may be key distractors. We bring mindful awareness to these, noticing how they are informing our moment, make wise adjustments accordingly, and let go so we can enjoy our food fully. Let's take a look at these factors, beginning with our mind.

Your Thoughts Affect Your Eating

Have you ever noticed how your thoughts affect your eating? Try sitting down and eating a meal with your full attention on each bite, chewing, swallowing, and enjoying. If you take the time to pay attention, you might notice how thoughts enter—of the future, things you need to do after your meal, the long list of unfinished business, planning for the week, happy memories perhaps associated with the food you are eating, or the setting you are eating in . . .

Each of these kinds of thoughts has the potential to affect your experience of eating, from subtle to very noticeable. You may rush through your meal because of thoughts of "all that you have to do" intruding upon your meal. You may notice your heart suddenly beats more quickly. You may notice you begin to eat faster, the rhythm of fork to mouth increasing perceptibly. Or you may notice a happy memory eliciting a sense of warmth and relaxation as you eat (this kind of thought can be nourishing, contributing positively to your experience). If you are having an anxious thought or worrying, you may find you are no longer enjoying the food and the taste has disappeared, unintentionally cast aside for indulging in the panoply of thoughts in your head.

Your Thoughts Affect Your Body

The fight-or-flight response is a very old mechanism in the body that evolved for our survival. When we perceive something to be a threat to our well-being—physically, emotionally, psychologically, or spiritually—our body responds by sending us a cascade of hormones that ready it for action, to fight or to flee the threat. The problem is that these days most threats to our well-being are not actually physical and can simply be the thoughts in our head. Our bodies don't know the difference between actual external physical threats and the thoughts that "threaten" our ease, our peace, our well-being. We react to thoughts in our head as well as actual stressors outside of ourselves.

So when you are enjoying your meal and these types of threatening thoughts arise, the stress response can get triggered. Cortisol and other stress hormones begin to circulate in the body. Unpleasant emotions can arise, barely perceived or uncomfortable. Blood flow gets diverted from the digestive system and other organs to the large muscle groups of the body to prepare you for action. In the realm of your mind, attention becomes diverted and focuses on the triggering thought and any other thoughts associated with it: "that deadline . . . I've got to get that email out immediately, or else . . ."

Poof! Any enjoyment of the meal gets hijacked. You may finish standing up, eating quickly, and moving on to the next task of the day. You may stay seated but are barely present for the rest of the meal. If you are lucky or have learned mindful eating techniques, you notice the thought, let it go on by, and come back to the full experience of eating.

Thoughts and the Digestion Connection

Some people react more strongly than others to stressors, both internal and external (such as a noisy environment, a challenging conversation, agitating media). Depending upon the perceived level of threat, your digestion may be affected. As blood flow gets diverted and the body gets the message that digestion is not that important right now, optimal levels of digestion decrease. Food may pass more quickly through your system, not fully absorbed, or your digestion may slow, causing discomfort or a stomachache. Other symptoms could include bloating, heartburn, and cramps.

The gut has a strong relationship with the brain. Neurotransmitter receptors in your gut are sensitive to emotional changes just as the brain is. This intuitive recognition is evidenced in our very language in expressions such as "I have a gut feeling," "I've received gut-wrenching news," "My gut reaction is . . ." Many digestive problems and symptoms are affected by emotions and stress, such as irritable bowel syndrome.

Nutrient absorption can also be affected by our state of mind as we eat. In fact research findings suggest that the more present you are to really taste and enjoy the pleasure of your food, the better you absorb your nutrients.

Scientists are recognizing more and more how your gut microbiome (the unique combination of bacteria that live in your gut) influences your health in many unexpected ways. More discoveries in the microbiota-gut-brain axis are made almost every month in this growing field. Conditions such as asthma, obesity, and even heart disease may be affected by your unique microbiome. Stress can reduce the number of beneficial bacteria in your gut, which can influence levels of gut inflammation, infection, weight gain or loss, and blood sugar levels.

Conversely, our microbiome itself can affect our mood. We don't yet understand fully how this occurs, but we do know that anxiety and depression are increased or reduced with certain gut flora. Gut bacteria produce neurotransmitters such as dopamine, GABA, and serotonin, which all play a key role in mood. Learning how to mindfully manage our thoughts, emotions, and stress while eating can help our digestion and our health.

Beliefs and Thought Stories Impact Your Eating

Besides the usual busyness of the mind that can take us away from being present to the nourishment from eating, common food thoughts directly affect the joy of eating. As you become more present to your thoughts and feelings as you eat, you may notice certain reoccurring beliefs. They may be so familiar, like a bad family of habits, that you barely notice them anymore. Or they may be so obvious and painful that you want to finally be free of them. They may feel like part of you. But they aren't. They are a repertoire of thoughts that have evolved from your unique life experiences, seasoned and influenced by family, friends, and societal and cultural values. They are not your fault! You didn't cause them.

Next time you eat a meal, notice what thoughts arise before, during, and after. What kinds of thoughts did you become aware of as you ate or prepared to eat? How are they affecting your experience of eating?

One common food belief is "I must finish the food on my plate," which is generally linked to childhood, when eating everything on your plate was a high priority for well-meaning parents. Their parents probably said the same thing, and there may have been very real issues of food scarcity in earlier generations. This adage is often followed by "because of the starving children in . . ."

I ask my clients who notice this belief, "Where is the most impactful waste? The 'waste' on the plate (that could go into compost) or the 'waist' that can grow from consistently eating extra food energy you don't need?" How much longer do you want to eat in a way that doesn't honor your body's fullness and satiety level? It can take time to lessen the behavioral impact of this belief, but you can do it with consistent, gentle awareness, feeling the discomfort but choosing to leave some food anyway.

Other common types of thoughts and beliefs that make it difficult to enjoy your meals in peace and experience optimum digestion include:

"This is a bad food—I shouldn't be eating it."

"Is this food really okay?"

"I'm a bad person for having two helpings."

"I blew it. I should never have had that slice of cake."

"Oh well—I may as well have the rest."

"This has a lot of calories. I shouldn't eat it at all, even though I really love this food."

Do you recognize any of these food thoughts or self-imposed rules? They can lead to inevitable feelings of guilt, negativity about yourself, helplessness, or just wanting to give up and overindulge again and again. Using mindfulness can help you let go of the agitating thoughts and come back to the simple practice of eating. You can see the thoughts for what they really are, just thoughts, the agitation they cause in the body, and the pure unhelpfulness of the contents. You can challenge the truth of the thoughts by using the techniques from chapter 6.

Thought-Emotion Connection

When you quiet the mind through mindfulness practice or simply pay attention, you will notice how a thought that passes through your mind can elicit an immediate emotional and physical response in the body: a feeling of anxiety, fear, stress, or anger and their associated physical sensations, tension, pressure, a twinge, faster heartbeat, tightness in the chest. Interestingly enough, it can go the other way too. Feelings may be affected by the food we eat, hormonal imbalances, physical stress response, insufficient sleep, lack of balance in the eight bodies of our lives, and, as we now know, even from imbalances in the gut microbiome.

We are meaning-making machines, seeking to understand and interpret our experience. When moods occur, we create thoughts or stories to explain those feelings. We look for what is not quite right in the moment, often choosing the most accessible explanation or compelling story and interpret the feeling with "nothing is going right for me right now because . . ." We may even overgeneralize or exaggerate the thoughts we have in those moments to "nothing is ever going right for me." These thoughts can perpetuate and even grow the feelings.

Mindfulness can help us see more clearly and not take our thoughts seriously all the time. It can help us let go more easily of the unhelpful thoughts and stories that impinge on our sense of well-being and balance. We can incline attention toward nourishing activities and unfold this new way of being at ease in the moment.

Life Circumstances

What are the kinds of life circumstances that get in the way of allowing food to fully nourish you? What takes your attention away from planning, preparing, and fully savoring your food? Deadlines, errands, emails, work, other responsibilities, emotional highs or lows all can seem more pressing and important at the time. Habitual eating with other activities and social situations can contribute to mindlessness. The intentions and goals you establish and prioritize in ensuing chapters to support your physical, social, and emotional bodies will help you to stay mindful no matter the life circumstances. By recalling your intentions, it will be easier to take actions that develop and maintain healthy habits.

Food Choices

Some foods are clearly more nourishing to our bodies than others. There are no nutritional advantages to consuming highly processed food—which usually contain large amounts of added sugar, salt, and saturated fat—except for brief pleasure, often followed by guilt! But with mindful eating we don't need to vilify the foods or ourselves if we eat them from time to time. We can put them in the category of sometimes foods versus always foods (healthy, nutrient-rich foods), rather than bad or good foods.

Our bodies thrive on whole, nutrient-rich, and predominantly plant-based foods—foods that are in their most natural state. The addition of highly processed foods to Western diets is linked to the chronic diseases that plague us today. In refined, highly processed carbohydrates, the germ, bran, and natural fiber that contain most of the vitamins, minerals, and protein are stripped away or discarded. What is left is the white starch devoid of any nutrients but empty calories.

When you eat whole-foods, plant-based diets, you are eating nutrient-rich foods. They provide you with a slow release of energy and the many nutrients that high-fiber diets offer. Fiber is an essential dietary component contributing to overall digestive health, colon health, healthy blood sugar control, and prevention of many chronic diseases. The even release of blood sugar gives you sustained energy throughout the day and helps to prevent the mood swings and irritability that can come with diets high in processed foods. Whole-foods, plant-based diets, which are inherently high in fiber, fortify your cells with the nutrients they need, giving you a deeper sense of nourishment. You can actually learn to tune in to this sense when you pay attention. Buy pesticide-free or organic produce when possible and visit the Environmental Working Group's (EWG.org) "dirty dozen foods to avoid" and "fifteen clean foods" to help guide you when to buy organic, or not.

High-sugar diets can give a quick jolt of energy and an immediate sense of gratification, but that rush is hollow and unsubstantiated without the foundational nutrition that our body needs. Mood swings, cravings, and irritability can result. Blood sugar levels can go up and down and promote insulin resistance if the swings are experienced frequently over time. Caffeine provides a similar input of energy by a very different mechanism. Both sugar and caffeine, if approached with moderation, mindfulness, and good nutrition practices, can generally be included in a sound eating plan. Wine enjoyed mindfully in moderate amounts may offer some health benefits, but of course too much can adversely affect health in the long run. Immediate effects could include headaches, dehydration, and poorer sleep. I always seem to have at least a few clients who are working on reducing their alcohol intake to one glass of wine with a meal or none at all, since more than a glass can lead to disinhibition, mindless overeating, and struggle.

Live raw foods, such as vegetables, nuts, and fruits, have the most life energy, especially the fresher the foods are and the more recently they have been picked. These foods absorb the energy of sunshine and have high levels of nutrients and enzymes undestroyed by cooking. Sprouted raw foods such as seeds, beans, whole grains and nuts offer even higher nutritional value. Raw foods have a different effect on your body than overcooked and processed foods. Most people do well with a combination of raw and cooked foods. The ideal proportion may vary as you change, grow, and age over the seasons.

Food Awareness Practice

Notice how different foods affect how you feel during, before, and after eating. What happens if you skip meals? Or ignore your hunger signals and end up eating even more later than you would have because you are so hungry? Record in your Well Nourished Journal what you notice over the period of a week. Use your observations to begin to guide your decisions.

Seven Tips to Mindful Eating Practice

Mindful eating enables us to experience greater pleasure and nourishment from our food. Through mindful awareness we become more attuned to our body's signals of pleasure, hunger, and fullness. We notice the food thoughts and beliefs that don't serve us and encourage those that do. We notice what is beneficial, nurturing these with our attention. We make choices that support our health and well-being and those of the planet. We practice kindness toward ourselves and our cravings and forgive ourselves for the difficult moments.

When we slow down, chew mindfully, and savor our food, we reduce stress, experience flavors fully, and improve digestion. When we focus on enjoying our food, worries fall away because we are no longer thinking about them. We tune in to and listen to signals from our body when we have had enough, thus helping us eat to a comfortable level rather than overeating.

Eating mindfully, with kindness, a nonjudging mind, and full awareness, can be learned and practiced daily with snacks and meals. I recommend beginning with just one snack or meal at first. Consider practicing when you are alone to make it easier to give your food your full attention, even if it's just for the first few bites. Notice when your mind has wandered and bring it back to the experience of eating as outlined in the seven tips below.

The steps to mindful eating are simple yet will take gentle and consistent practice. With time they will become a conscious habit. You can actually come to the point where you are eating mindfully most of the time and don't have to work to remember. But realistically no one stays present with eating all of the time. It's a practice to return to again and again, just a breath and a bite away. Ultimately, mindful eating can be practiced at different paces to be part of your life with the varied situations you will inevitably encounter. Mindful eating is flexible and can become part of your life—whether you have a busy family or live alone.

Following the seven tips will help you begin to cultivate your own mindful eating practice. Although all the tips are presented here, we'll focus on cultivating nourishment and pleasure first. In chapter 4 we'll take a deeper dive into the subtleties of hunger, fullness, and taste awareness and how they help moderate quantity.

First, the Brief Version

To begin with we always practice slowing down the process of eating. Take a few mindful breaths to become centered and present. Feast on the sight, colors, and textures of the food. Breathe in the aroma of the food. Take a moment if you'd like to feel a sense of gratitude for the food in front of you and reflect on where the food came from and what went into making that food, such as the people, the earth, the sunshine. Tune in to your hunger and fullness level before and several times during the meal to help guide you to eat the right amount for you during the meal. Savor the taste and texture as you eat and chew fully before swallowing. Stop when you are comfortably full or satisfied.

The Seven Tips

1. ***Take a Mindful Check-In.*** Before or during a snack or meal, bring your awareness to your breath, pause, and then notice any thoughts or feelings that may be present, particularly any in relation to the food you are about to eat. This may be just a brief moment or up to a couple of minutes. It is the first step to increasing awareness, releasing any potential reactivity that may be present, and raising the possibility of true nourishment.

Begin by taking a few deep, relaxing breaths. Now simply tune in to the movement of your in breath and out breath. Expand your awareness to include the whole of your body and notice without judgment what thoughts, feelings, and body sensations are present. Note how this may inform your choices about how much, when, and what to eat, and desires or cravings for food. Practice this at least once a day to begin with. Eventually it will become a more conscious habit.

The Mindful Check-In begins the mindful eating practice but will also be a foundational stand-alone practice that we will visit again throughout the chapters in various capacities.

2.   ***Check in with your hunger and fullness level before eating.*** While practicing your Mindful Check-In, tune in to your level of physical hunger. We enjoy our food the most when we have some hunger or are moderately hungry. When we are too hungry we tend to eat fast and even overeat.

Ask yourself, How hungry am I? Listen to the sensations and experiences that your body is giving you. Is this physical hunger or something else? If it's not physical hunger (and you will get better at discerning this), ask yourself, What am I really hungry for?

Tune in to your level of physical fullness. Ask yourself, How full am I? Listen to the sensations and experiences that your body is giving you. If you are full, then eating right now would probably not be a very kind or nourishing choice. What kinds of choices make sense with what you became aware of? What would most honor your body?

3.   ***Gaze at the food and take a moment to reflect upon it.*** How did the food get to you, what went into making it, who and what were involved (people, sun, earth, water, farmers)? Consider the quality and sources. Feel a sense of appreciation or gratitude for the food before you.

4.   ***Enjoy your food with all your senses.***
~ Feast your eyes visually on the food. Notice color, texture, shape.
~ *Smell* the food, breathing in the aroma, noticing the nuances with both nostrils.
~ *Taste* the food, first savoring without chewing it, noticing the flavor, texture, and sensations.

~ Then *chew* the food, staying as present as possible with each bite to fully enjoy the experience.

~ Mindfully *swallow* when ready.

Notice any associations that arise, whether pleasant or unpleasant. Bask in any pleasant associations or positive memories if you'd like, while still staying present with the full experience.

5. **Taste mindfully.** Pay attention to the taste, savoring fully, noticing when it diminishes and when enjoyment lessens. Use this awareness to help inform decisions about how much and how little to eat, when to stop, and when to eat more, as is helpful. This can help particularly with moderating the amount of highly processed foods.

6. **Check in with hunger and fullness levels occasionally throughout the snack or meal.** Refer to number 2. Use these to guide when you have had enough.

7. **Practice, practice, practice.** At first we eat slowly when we practice mindful eating. The slow pace can be likened to the training wheels we use to learn to ride a bike. As we become more practiced and hone our attention skills, mindful eating becomes more natural. We can learn to eat mindfully not only slowly but at different paces, settings, alone and with others.

With attuned awareness we can eat in a way that becomes satisfying, guilt- and struggle-free, and with the quantities and quality that support our optimum health and well-being.

Visit Your Destination

Let's take a quick trip to the future and see what it looks like when you are practicing mindful eating. Imagine that you know the foods that your body thrives on. You have paid attention to what your body loves, to the foods and way of eating that give you the greatest sense of well-being, energy, clarity, and balance. You have learned to pay attention to when you are hungry, comfortably full, and when your body feels satisfied. You've learned to differentiate this from what your mind wants.

You tune in to the taste of food and enjoy it with all your senses. You feel connected to the food, where it came from, and the life energy it brings to you. You have educated yourself on sound nutrition principles and understand the benefits and disadvantages of different approaches. You are able to know and honor what your body wants and needs, rather than consistently overriding it with your mind. You have created a strong overall intention that keeps you aligned with your highest goals for well-being. You come back to this again and again as you navigate the many food and self-care choices that present themselves each day. You plan ahead and listen to what your body is calling for, now able to discern which part of you is truly hungry. You make a mindful choice and have an ongoing plan to nourish each of the bodies that make up your whole self. Buckle your seat belt and follow that compass to your destination.

Balancing Inner and Outer Nourishment

CHAPTER THREE

A Map to Your Well-Nourished Life: Mindfulness and the 5 Steps

You can shine the light of your awareness on each area of your life to discern what you truly need.

Learning how to eat and live in a way that can truly nourish our whole selves is foundational. What we take in and how well the body is able to process it directly affect our health and state of being. Throughout the rest of this book we will explore how you can nourish yourself, and how this in turn supports the practice and cultivation of mindful eating. Learning to discern what you are truly hungry for, having the skills and tools to give to yourself in a graceful and mindful way, and to sustain this way of living doesn't happen without support and knowledge. This chapter offers the framework we will use in the book and beyond. We do this not only for ourselves; the more deeply fulfilled we are, the more we naturally want to give back to others, to the community, and to the world.

Each of the ensuing chapters introduces an important body, or part of your whole self: physical, emotional, psychological, social, intellectual, creative, spiritual, and worldly. As you read, you will have an opportunity to bring awareness to how well fed you are in each of these areas and assess what "essential nutrients" might be missing. You'll be introduced to information about each body and how to use your own inner knowing as well to set intentions for yourself in each of these areas. *Skills and tools* will be introduced to help you implement your intentions in your life. You'll learn how to cultivate *outer support* and *inner resources* to keep you on track.

We've broken down this framework into 5 steps.

5 Steps to Mindful Eating and Living

1. Awareness   3. Skills and Tools   5. Inner Resources

2. Intention   4. Outer Support

AWARENESS

The first step to any change is awareness: realizing that the way you have been doing things, nourishing yourself, being in the world, or feeling and thinking is not your ideal. You know intuitively you can do better, live better, be better. You are doing things the same way over and over, or perhaps you are even trying some new things, but they are producing the same result in your life.

We can see our lives most clearly when we practice mindfulness, the nonjudging and compassionate way of viewing the present moment, ourselves, and all of our experiences. In the last chapter we explored how you can bring mindful attention to the way you eat and transform your relationship to the experience of eating. Resting your attention fully in the present moment allows you to better recognize the patterns and habits you fall back on and enables you to make choices that are free of automaticity. Practicing mindful awareness opens the door to experiencing the peace and spaciousness that are available to you as you identify with awareness the unchanging part of you, rather than overidentifying with the changing nature of your thoughts, feelings, struggles, and experiences. This helps free you from the part of yourself that struggles with food and eating and opens up the space to make true change.

We can begin to cultivate mindfulness by practicing both formally and informally. Learning and practicing the art of mindfulness meditation on a daily basis helps support the successful practice of mindful eating and living. It polishes the lens of our awareness so we can see more clearly what is really true in each moment, honoring our thoughts, emotions, and desires.

You can shine the light of your awareness on each area of your life to discern what you need overall and in each moment. What are you truly hungry for? In the beginning of each chapter, as part of the Awareness step, you will be asked some basic questions to evaluate each area of your life—to pause, reflect, and assess. This process will give you both a bird's-eye view and a view from within. What areas in your life are missing nourishment and would most benefit from changing? What is important to you? Are you seeking nourishment through food because a particular area is overlooked or neglected, while yet another is overemphasized? These are the types of questions that will be posed in this mini-assessment. You'll take a moment to pause, perhaps take several relaxing breaths, and reflect upon the questions.

As you finish your Awareness step, you will be prompted to do a Mindful Check-In so you can dig a little deeper. This involves taking a few intentional breaths and focusing on the sensations of the breath. As you ask yourself the series of questions, bring your awareness to the whole of your body, noticing what is arising, your sensations, feelings, and thoughts, as you answer. Feel free to write down your answers if that helps with your assessment.

When you are assessing each area of your life under a lens, it may be easy to judge yourself negatively or jump to conclusions. Judgment can make the filter cloudy and leave you with unpleasant feelings. Each time you sense any judgment arising, simply see it for what it is—a thought that you don't have to believe. You may label it "judgment" and let go of it as you bring your attention back to reflecting on the assessment questions. You may direct a sense of compassion and kindness toward any thoughts that are not helpful or are self-sabotaging. You may even "talk back" to negative thoughts that arise.

Perhaps you are aware of a thought such as "you can never change this" or "you don't have enough time." Counter gently with a wiser self that is bigger than those habitual thoughts, the self that bought this book and is committed to making changes: "I will be able to make changes one step at a time"; "I am learning tools and practices that will help me prioritize and make wise use of my time." You can always come back to your overall intention, which you established in chapter 1. It can be helpful to pause, take a few mindful breaths, and gently repeat your intention to yourself.

Approaching the inquiries in this way will help you see more clearly and accurately and lead to a more enjoyable and enlightening process. When we are not stuck in our judgments or usual way of seeing things, new possibilities, solutions, and insights can emerge. Our intentions can come together more effortlessly, and resistances we have to fully implementing them can be explored mindfully. Along with the awareness you gain from looking deeply into your own experience, you can use the information offered in each chapter to help create your specific intention(s) for that body, and ultimately the clear goals that will help you move toward your desired state of nourishment in each area of your life.

INTENTION

The overall intention that you chose in chapter 1 has set your direction for crafting your well-nourished life. Your intention can lead the way, like a vibrating heartstring or resonant tuning fork. You just need to remember to listen and come back to it as a touchstone. It can be helpful in the midst of so many choice points in daily life.

Now you will set individual intentions for each body, followed by specific goals (at the end of each chapter) to take them out into action. You can balance the key information in each area with wisdom from your own experience to help create your intentions and goals. Both will be important guideposts that keep you moving on the larger track of a well-nourished life. Your commitment to your intentions and goals can be informed not only by what you become aware of but by understanding the importance of taking care of your whole self.

Your intentions and goals will help you successfully integrate and incorporate these new, rediscovered, or re-remembered ingredients of a fulfilling life. The skills and tools you learn will help support your intentions and may be the very ingredients you choose to nourish yourself as well.

Steps to Setting Intentions and Goals

Remember to put your intention into positive language and the present moment as if it is occurring now. Alternatively it may be a positive wish of well-being for yourself. You might write a longer intention and then have a short version to remember in the moment when faced with myriad choices throughout each day.

For example, you can create an intention around the basic practice of mindful eating that resonates for you. These might include:

~ I would like to practice eating mindfully most of the time (for my health and well-being).

~ I intend to develop a practice of mindful eating.

~ I am open to this new way of eating and nourishment for my body.

~ May I experience joy and nourishment from the food that I eat.

~ May I let go of struggling with the food I choose to eat.

~ May I let go of my concepts about food and eating that do not serve me.

~ May I allow mindful eating to nourish my body.

Your intention will guide you toward noticing the circumstances, people, and things that will support you, maybe even in unexpected ways. It's as if you are energetically drawn toward all that you need, and it is being drawn to you.

With more knowledge, skills, and tools, you will create a more specific goal to put your intention into action at the end of each chapter using a goal-setting tool called SPRIGS (which stands for Specific, Positive, Realistic, Inspiring (and Desirable), Grounded in Time/Gaugeable, and Set Your Next Step).

Setting Goals with SPRIGS

A sprig is a small stem that bears leaves, buds, and flowers. As each sprig blossoms and bears fruit, it contributes to a larger thriving bush or tree. By setting goals using the SPRIGS method, you create a way to enhance your intention.

Your goals should be:

S: Specific

P: Positive

R: Realistic

I: Inspiring

G: Grounded in Time and Gaugeable and finally, allow you to:

S: Set Your Next Steps

Mindfulness and awareness help us tune in moment to moment, stay in our center, and discern what is the right action for us. Our intention and goals help guide the way. Mindfulness practices and other skills and tools provide specific means to realize our intentions and put them into action.

A variety of skills and tools drawing upon evidence-based practices, such as applied neuroscience, mindfulness, behavioral science, health education, and cognitive-behavioral techniques, and ancient wisdom practices and spiritual traditions from across cultures are offered in each chapter to help you focus your intentions and reach your goals. Some of these will support you to stay on track; some of these will actually be part of your goals. In other words, the ingredients you have incorporated into your goals may include the very skills and tools that comprise your well-nourished and mindful life.

SPRIGS: Put Your Intention into Action

Set your SPRIGS goal, using any skills and tools to work toward your intention. For example, let's say the specific skill and ingredient you choose is the basic mindful eating practice.

Your intention: *I would like to practice eating mindfully most of the time.*

The skill: *basic mindful eating practice*

You'll now create a very specific goal to put some legs on your intention to help it manifest practically using the skill(s) you choose. Following SPRIGS, you will:

S—Specific. Make your goal specific by addressing what, why, how, where, and when. "I am going to practice eating at least one snack or meal mindfully each day using the basic mindful eating instructions. I will practice at home in the morning when it is quiet and I am alone." Link the why to your larger intention in this example: "to develop a practice of mindful eating."

P—Positive. Check that your goal is a positive action step, a call to action, not what you aren't going to do.

R—Realistic. Check that it is realistic and attainable for you. That it's not too much to ask for in your schedule nor too substantial to carry out in the given time.

I—Inspiring (and Desirable). Check that you've chosen a goal that is inspiring and desirable to you, a step in the direction of your specific intention. Add reasons why, to make it more compelling and connected to your intention. These may include statements connecting it to both your intention for mindful eating and your overall intention. Some examples of inspiring and motivating reasons that support your goal could include:

> ~ *This is helping me learn to eat in a way that is calmer and healthier for my body. I'm tuning in to the amounts and quality of food that my body really needs.*
>
> ~ *I am tuning in to what I really need, which may not include more servings of food or any food at all.*
>
> ~ *I'm learning to eat in a way that is energizing, satisfying, and promotes a sense of well-being after a meal.*
>
> ~ *I am learning to eat to just what my body needs, while enjoying each bite.*
>
> ~ *I am learning to eat in a way that really nourishes me.*

G—Grounded in Time and Gaugeable. Ground your goal in the real world by adding another time component, such as when you are going to start. This makes it even more specific. For example, I'm going to start on Monday after my houseguests leave. I plan to practice at breakfast. If I am not able to or forget to practice at breakfast, I will choose another meal or snack that day.

You can ground the specific goal in time with an end point as well. Ask yourself how long you are going to practice this goal. You can use both subjective and objective measures of success to determine when it may be time to adjust your goal. For example, a more subjective measure would be when eating a meal mindfully becomes relatively easy to remember and practice; more objective, when you have one specific meal you eat mindfully each day, such as breakfast.

Gauge your goal. Check in with how you are doing from time to time. Choose a daily, weekly, or monthly check-in time with yourself. Did you reach your goal? Are you on track to your satisfaction? Do you feel a certain amount of ease, competency, and familiarity? Is it still inspiring, desirable, or realistic to you? Has anything changed in your life circumstances where you may need to adjust your expectations either up or down?

With this step you can gauge when you are ready to increase mindful eating practice to the next level using the measures you set. Even if you practice for only a small part of that meal—at the beginning, middle, or end—you may choose to consider that a success.

Life is not always linear. Your experiences can vary depending on your perception and how mindful you are. At times, the way you gauge your goal's success may be more subjective than objective, and that is perfectly fine. The more mindful you become, the more inner and outer experiences will help you determine your next steps, and your experience of time may feel more seamless. You may find yourself incorporating new lifestyle habits without strictly employing a linear form of goal setting. It may be a more intuitive process. And at the same time it may keep you moving on a steady track.

S—Set Your Next Steps. Once you feel you have achieved your goal to your satisfaction, consider, What are your next steps? Will you make it more challenging? Will you choose a different goal in this area to move toward your intentions?

OUTER SUPPORT

Research shows that having a buddy or social support around your goals or during changes in your life makes a positive difference. Look at your life and the people in it. Are there sources of support you can draw upon? Support might come from one or more friends, family members, a community, a coach, a therapist, a clergyperson, or other guide. You could create a check-in system with yourself and others by asking a buddy to be a check-in partner for support around your new goals. Having a regular time to evaluate how each of you is doing with your own individual goals is invaluable and proven to reduce stress. It can ease the way and be more fun and effective. You can check in weekly by text, email, or phone.

You could also join a group, start a group, or become part of a group of volunteers that share the same values or intentions. I have check-in buddies to keep me accountable in different aspects of my life, and several different groups that nourish my work, creative, and spiritual life. I have friends and family to share nature with and many other activities that are uplifting to my heart and soul.

Feeling isolated and lacking social connection can contribute to depression and low motivation. Finding ways to stay connected and involved keeps you more engaged in life while sharing energy, inspiration, and motivation with like-minded people. Specific suggestions will be offered in the ensuing chapters for ways to engage outer support for each "body" of the whole self.

Outer Support can also include using the structure of the goal-setting tool SPRIGS, environmental props, or supports such as strategically posted reminder notes and setting timers. For instance, in our SPRIGS example above, eating one meal or snack mindfully each day, you might set your phone timer to a lovely chime to remind you to pause and enjoy your breakfast mindfully. If for some reason you're not able to that morning, you could reset it to eat mindfully a late-afternoon healthy snack or another meal. (Through awareness and assessment you might have come to realize an afternoon snack is important to include in your day so you won't be too ravenous during preparation of the family dinner and end up overeating.) You could also invite a friend to practice eating a snack mindfully with you.

INNER RESOURCES

The practices offered throughout the book cultivate an inner ground of nourishment. These include mindfulness, self-compassion and compassion, gratitude and appreciation, joy and kindness toward yourself and others. Many of these are discussed in chapters 5 and 6. Here is a sneak preview of self-compassion and gratitude practice.

Self-Compassion

Cultivating a voice of compassion for yourself as you navigate the way to a well-nourished life can make all the difference in staying motivated and feeling at ease. It's especially helpful when you encounter moments where your actions or life's circumstances don't meet your expectations, your judging mind is active, or you are simply hurting. Studies show that people practicing self-compassion have less anxiety and depression. The mind becomes quieter and more peaceful as distressed, repetitive, worry-filled thinking is reduced. Caring for oneself becomes easier. Self-compassion strengthens self-accountability and initiation of positive steps in your life as you simply begin to care about and value yourself more.

Gratitude and Appreciation

A regular practice of eliciting gratitude—taking time out to appreciate and be thankful for all that you have and all that you are—can nourish your life immensely and keep you motivated. Gratitude practice increases positive emotions, including joy, optimism, and happiness. Those who practice feel less lonely or isolated and are more apt to better care for themselves and others. With gratitude practice you can regularly celebrate your life and accomplishments, not just the big things in life but even the small, ordinary details of everyday life, while appreciating the miracle of life in its simplicity and grand mystery. You can feel grateful and appreciative for your very efforts to live a fulfilled life. This reinforces being right on course and helps you feel nourished exactly where you are. For example, imagine you are taking the time to notice, savor, and appreciate your mindful eating practice. You are engaging nonjudgmental awareness to appreciate that you are practicing each day. You are inclining your mind toward the good, what is positive, and what is working. You focus on that, soaking it in, rather than focusing on what you didn't do that day.

When you aren't able to practice, you are forgiving and kind with yourself. In the past you might have beaten yourself up with a plethora of judgments for not meeting your expectations. You are celebrating the small steps you practiced this day—even if they weren't quite meeting your full goal. You look forward instead to the imminent opportunities to practice that will naturally unfold in your life. You guide your attention to notice these.

Engaging the tools of inner support helps cultivate your ground of nourishment. Each time you use these tools, you are watering the seeds you've planted. They can grow and flourish in proportion to the attention you pay to them.

Bringing awareness to these 5 steps on a regular basis can keep us inspired, waking up grateful, appreciative, self-reflective, self-responsible, and energized. They provide a framework to engage tools and a master plan that keeps us alert and living a conscious and well-nourished life—if we choose to use them.

In the next eight chapters you will have the opportunity to use these 5 steps as a template for making sustainable changes.

Use Mindfulness as a Tool

Mindful awareness is fundamental to mindful eating and living. It informs all of the 5 steps. We will focus on the cultivation of mindful awareness through some foundational practices and see how this important tool can help us with the first step, Awareness.

Cultivate Mindful Awareness

Mindfulness offers a clear, nonjudging, and compassionate way of being in and viewing the present moment. You can use this way of being and seeing, sometimes called "beginner's mind," to look at your own life in a fresh new way. The practice of mindfulness meditation can help you cultivate this awareness and bring it to the moments of your life. The more you practice, the more you remember to remember. Mindfulness becomes more effortless, dare we say, a new habit? It certainly becomes a new way of being.

Sitting meditation is a wonderful training ground for this practice, but you can practice mindfulness without formally meditating throughout the day. The key is to practice intentionally, nonjudgmentally, with kindness, paying attention to your experience, thoughts, feelings, and physical sensations without reacting, without attaching, clinging to, or pushing away what you encounter.

We have already discussed some mindful eating tools in chapter 2. These include:

> ~ *Food awareness practice.* Notice how different foods affect how you feel during, before, and after eating.
>
> ~ *Mindful eating practice.* Pay attention with all your senses, with kindness, nonjudging mind, and full awareness.

For the first week or so focus on:

step 1. *Mindful Check-In: Before eating a snack or meal, take a moment to bring your awareness to your breath, pause, and notice any thoughts or feelings that may be present, particularly any in relation to the food you are about to eat. How do they inform your experience of eating?*

step 2. *Gaze at the food and take a moment to reflect upon how the food got to you. Elicit a sense of gratitude and appreciation.*

step 3. *Enjoy your food with all your senses.*

step 4. *Pay attention to your body's cues when it has had enough.*

Now let's consider additional mindfulness practices.

Practice Mindfulness

Mindfulness meditation with breath as the main focus of awareness becomes easier with practice. A sense of peace and calm can arise during practice and be more accessible during the day. You can develop the ability to be more present, and your moments can become more vivid and rich. Just as important, you are cultivating your mindfulness muscle, your ability to pay attention to the changing nature of your experience, moment to moment, with greater kindness and nonjudgment, without attaching and getting lost in nonhelpful beliefs and strong emotions. This allows the freedom and space to make choices that best support your deepest intentions.

The fundamental practices that will support mindful eating and living are *mindfulness meditation* and *mindful awareness*. The following support the cultivation of mindful awareness. Other mindful practices specific to each chapter will be introduced throughout this book.

Choose one or more of these to begin practicing at least once daily.

Mindfulness of Daily Activities. Try paying attention mindfully to routine activities such as walking, driving, washing, or drinking tea using the activity itself as your main focus. Notice the sensation of your feet touching the ground as you walk down the sidewalk. How do you feel as you dip your hands in the sudsy dishwater? Focus on the aroma of your tea as you take a sip.

General Mindful Check-In. Use a Mindful Check-In at any moment of the day. It is particularly helpful to use before eating or during challenging moments. Take a few intentional breaths focusing on the sensations of the breath. Begin to broaden your awareness in other moments of your day, to the whole of your body, noticing what is arising, your reactions, bodily sensations, feelings, and thoughts. What is happening? How is what you are aware of informing your moment? Take a few more mindful breaths. Did you gain perspective? Feel calmer? Are there actions you are taking or would like to take? The check-in can take less than a minute or be a little longer.

You can practice mindful awareness at various times throughout the day. It can be helpful to rest your attention lightly on your breathing or another part of your body, such as the soles of your feet, to help you stay present. Practice an attitude of kindness to whatever your experience is and come back gently to the moment and/or activity you are focusing on.

Sitting Meditation.

Time of Day and Place: It is best to find a regular time each day to habituate this wonderful self-care practice of daily meditation. Morning when you first get up is often an ideal time. The mind is usually quieter at this time of day, and you can set the tone for your day by getting in the practice early. Lunchtime or late afternoon after work can also be a good time. Experiment with different times to find the one that works best for you and your schedule. Choose a place where you won't be disturbed. If you live with others, let them know you'll be practicing. Put pets in a different room if you think they will bother you.

Sitting Posture: Choose a chair or cushion.

Chair: Sit in a chair that is comfortable yet firm to medium soft with a relatively straight back. Feet should be able to reach flat on the floor. If they don't reach, you may put a pillow or book between your feet and the floor. Sit with a straight back away from the back of the chair to help you keep alert yet relaxed. If you need the support of the back of the chair you may use it, sitting in a comfortable upright posture.

Cushion: Sit cross-legged on a cushion or two such that your hips are higher than your knees. This allows the lower back to be in a comfortable, natural, more straight alignment. Alternatively, you may have your knees folded, lower legs resting on either side of the cushion.

Length: If you are new to meditation, you may want to try ten minutes of practice the first few times. As you get more comfortable, increase up to twenty to thirty minutes a day. You may choose to go longer if you like. Make the practice your own, finding the length of time that will help you be most successful.

The Practice: Find a position that feels comfortable on your chair or cushion and with a minimum of strain on the back. Hands rest comfortably on your lap folded, or palms rest up or down on your thighs. Take a few deep breaths through the nose to begin with allowing the breath to flow all the way down to the belly and out again. Breathe in again, bringing awareness to the sensations of breath in the body as you do so. Repeat a few times. Now allow the breath to return to its normal and natural rhythm. Find a place to rest attention on the breath that feels easy and comfortable. It may be at the tip of the nose, chest, or belly, or along the entire course of breath. Let this be your anchor, resting your attention on the breath. When you notice your mind has wandered away from the breath, simply note where attention has gone (e.g., to thoughts, feelings, body sensations, or sounds) without engaging, without judgment and gently come back to the breath.

Return to the breath again and again each time the mind wanders. (You may find that what your attention was drawn to fades away to the background and then simply dissipates.) When a thought arises again, you repeat the process, coming back to the breath, practicing kind, nonjudgmental awareness. Let thoughts, feelings, physical sensations, sounds simply be in the space of your awareness when you notice them, without engaging or struggling against them, and then return gently back to the breath. Breath becomes predominant in your attention once again. Continue to rest in kind awareness of the breath.

Yogic Breath

For deeper relaxation and concentration, try this yogic breath at the beginning of your meditation. Allow the breath to flow all the way down into the stomach, then fill the area of the ribs and finally the chest. Exhale slowly, reversing the movement of breath out, relaxing the chest, ribs, and finally releasing the stomach.

Decide upon the amount of time you would like to practice. Set a timer with a pleasant sound or meditation bell app to ring at the end of your designated period.

Ways to Use the Book:
Worksheets and Prompters

As you move through each of the eight following chapters, using the 5 steps and mindfulness practices, you'll bring awareness to each area, asking yourself how developed and nourished each particular "body" in your life is. Is there anything missing here? Is what you are hungry for or needing in the moment not actually food, but to feed this part of yourself in a nonfood way?

Once you've set your intentions and learned more about each area, what are the specific skills and tools to help you reach your goals? What are the quality ingredients you want to include? Many sprigs (SPRIGS) make up the beautiful, thriving tree of your life. Use the tools of inner and outer support to help water and nurture your goals.

The following prompter tools for the 5 steps can help you to stay on track. These are important tools that we'll call upon throughout the book, so let's review each carefully. (For additional copies, visit www.yourwellnourishedlife.com.)

5 Steps Prompter Tools

1. ***Intention and Goals Prompter (pages 56, 58 and 59)***
   As you go through each chapter, fill in each step in this prompter to remind you of your intentions, goals, skills you are using, and support you'll need to reach

them. When you have satisfactorily integrated the goal into your life, or would like to work on new skills and tools, you can reassess and adjust as you like. Use one prompter for each "body."

2. **5 Steps Daily Prompter: In the Moment (page 57)**

Refer to this Daily Prompter sheet during the day to help you stay mindful in the moment. After a while you likely will not need it, as mindfully checking in will become a new positive habit. The Daily Prompter may be especially helpful during times of transition, emotional stress, challenges, or traveling.

Always begin with a Mindful Check-In to see what you really need *(Am I physically hungry? What do I really need? What is my true need in this moment? Can I give that to myself right now?)*.

Mindfulness Prompters

As we use Intention and Goals Prompters for the 5 steps in each chapter, we will utilize prompters for our mindfulness practices. Mindfulness and mindful eating each have their own intention prompter sheet, as they are so fundamental, in addition to the prompter sheets used for each "body."

WELL NOURISHED INTENTION AND GOALS PROMPTER

Body: *(e.g., physical, emotional, creative, etc.)* _____

Intention: _____

_____

_____

Skills and Tools

_____

_____

_____

_____

Your SPRIGS Goals
(Specific, Positive, Realistic, Inspiring, Grounded in Time/Gaugeable, Set Next Step)

1. Outer Support

_____

_____

2. Inner Resources

_____

_____

Journal Notes: *(e.g., I notice when I have good food in the house, it's so much easier to eat healthy lunches during the day; I'm going to plan my schedule better for shopping trips.)*

_____

_____

_____

_____

WELL NOURISHED 5 STEPS DAILY PROMPTER

Daily Well Nourished Check-In *(use in the moments throughout your day)*	5 Steps to Mindful Eating and Living *(use daily, weekly, monthly, anytime)*
Mindful Check-In: Am I physically hungry?_____ What is my true need in this moment? _____ Can I give that to myself right now? _____	*Awareness* ~ Do a Mindful Check-In to assess your true level of physical hunger. ~ Notice your thoughts, feelings, physical sensations. ~ Discern your true need.
Use Your Intentions: Overall:_____ For this body: _____ New intention (optional): _____	*Intention* ~ Call in overall intention to stay on track ~ Call in "body" intention for that need ~ Set a new situational intention (optional)
Nourish Yourself: ~ Choose Skills and Tools to help you. ~ Make a plan with a SPRIGS if helpful. ~ Fill in your Bowl (see page 60).	*Skills and Tools* (e.g., mindful breathing, nourishing activity, SPRIGS) _____ _____ _____
Choose Outer Support as needed. *(e.g., check-in buddy, SPRIGS)* _____ _____ _____	*Outer Support* (e.g., check-in buddy, SPRIGS)
Choose Inner Resources as needed. *(e.g., self-compassion, lovingkindness, meditation)* _____ _____ _____	*Inner Resources* (e.g., self-compassion, lovingkindness, meditation)

WELL NOURISHED INTENTION AND GOALS PROMPTER

Mindfulness Intention:

_____

_____

_____

Skills and Tools

_____

_____

_____

_____

Your SPRIGS Goals
(Specific, Positive, Realistic, Inspiring, Grounded in Time/Gaugeable, Set Next Step)

1. Outer Support

_____

_____

2. Inner Resources

_____

_____

Journal Notes: *(e.g., It is getting easier to practice sitting meditation each day after three weeks. I actually look forward to it. I can get quiet, focused, and calm more easily. During the day I am less reactive to others. I'm pausing and making better choices in both my eating and how I respond to family members.)*

_____

_____

_____

_____

WELL NOURISHED INTENTION AND GOALS PROMPTER

Mindful Eating Intention: _____
_____
_____

Skills and Tools

_____
_____
_____
_____

Your SPRIGS Goals
(Specific, Positive, Realistic, Inspiring, Grounded in Time/Gaugeable, Set Next Step)

1. Outer Support

_____
_____

2. Inner Resources

_____
_____

Journal Notes: *(e.g., The Mindful Check-In before eating is helping me be more aware of what I really need and want. I'm making healthier food choices. I love pausing and appreciating the food before I eat. I'm enjoying my food so much more.)*

_____
_____
_____
_____
_____

Your Well Nourished Bowl

This bowl is a metaphor for your life. Each petal represents a body. The outer circle represents the nourishing container of mindfulness and lovingkindness that you will be cultivating. Lovingkindness is an attitude of kindness, friendliness, and love that will be fully introduced in chapter 5. As your read each chapter, use this bowl for a reminder and inspiration. Fill in each petal corresponding to the body with the nourishment you choose—the skills, tools, and activities you are adding to nourish each body. Visit www.yourwellnourishedlife.com to download a larger reusable version of this bowl.

YOUR WELL NOURISHED BOWL

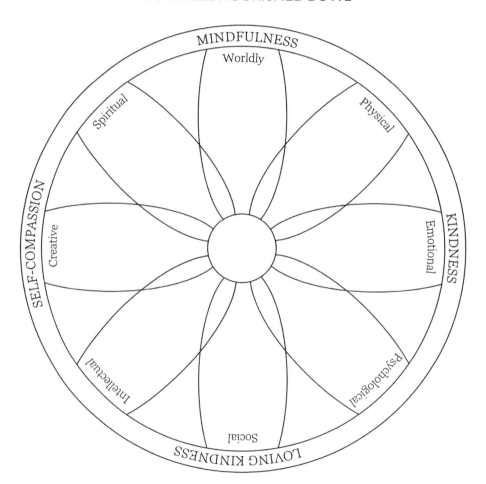

Not all the areas you assess will hold the same value and importance for you as others. You are your own master chef. You may find you are undernourished in some areas and thus want to take particular steps to achieve better balance. Conversely, you may determine that an area lower in nourishment isn't as high a priority for you as another.

Setting Your Course

There are different ways you can choose your approach to this book, depending on what makes sense for you as discussed in the introduction. If you decide to read through the entire book first, do the Awareness and Intention steps, and then go back to apply the rest of the 5 steps in each chapter. It will be helpful to prioritize what areas are most important to you, what will make the most difference in your life, and what to focus on. You will have more success if you are not trying to do everything at once.

The first step in prioritizing is working through your intentions to determine which bodies to focus on.

1. Write your overall intention (established in chapter 1) on the top of a blank page.

2. Next, write headings for each of the eight bodies (physical, emotional, etc.), then list your specific intentions for each below your overall intention, which is your destination. Group any intentions together if you write more than one for a body.

3. Prioritize the bodies by first reflecting on these questions:
   ~ Which ones call to you?
   ~ Which ones do you feel more energy and excitement about?
   ~ Which might make the most immediate or biggest impact on your total well-being?
   ~ Which will you choose to focus on first to move closer to your overall intention?
   Based on your answers, rank each body from one to eight, with one being the most important, and eight being the least important or compelling. There is no right or wrong to how you choose.

4. Choose the three areas that you rated most important. These will be the bodies you'll increase nourishment in first. If the physical body is not one of them, yet is an area that is "undernourished," consider including aspects of the physical body such as nutrition, exercise, or sleep in your intentions, as these cornerstones of mindful eating and living.

Ready for Practical Action: Less not More

Successful long-term lifestyle change usually comes from making changes slowly over time. It's easy to feel overwhelmed. You don't have to do everything at once or read through the entire book in one sitting. Then you might be more likely to give up or not begin at all. Remain aware of your overall intention and the areas of your life that you want to nourish. As you become more satisfied with using the 5 steps, you can add more areas in your life to focus upon, or further enrich those you are already focusing on.

CHAPTER FOUR

Physical Nourishment: Maintaining a Healthy Lifestyle

Our body is precious. It is our vehicle for awakening.
Treat it with care. —Buddha

Your body is like a veritable temple housing your soul, your essential self in this life. Without the good health of the physical body, nourishing the other parts of yourself becomes harder. It is essential that we start at the physical level to make our foundation strong. So much goes into having a healthy physical body: good food in moderate amounts, water, sleep, exercise, movement, rest, healthy pleasures and relaxation, and love. To bring awareness to this important area you will assess the quality and level of these essential ingredients.

As in the other chapters that discuss the "bodies," we'll use the 5 steps beginning with Awareness and Intention to assess how well you are taking care of your physical body, focusing on nutrition and mindful eating but also considering exercise and movement, sleep, and rest and relaxation. We'll look at pertinent information and the Skills and Tools you can use to make concrete changes where needed. (Love and emotional connection also nourish the physical body, but we'll save that for a later chapter.)

Essential Ingredients

Diet and nutrition impact our direct experience of physical, mental, and emotional well-being more than most of us realize—not only the types of food we eat but how we eat, when we eat, the quality of what we eat, and how much we eat. Our body immediately uses what we take in for energy and nutrients, so that what we eat becomes the building blocks of our body. Food can affect how we feel physically, our energy level, our moods, focus, and attention.

Movement is essential to the health of any body, from the cellular to the macroscopic level. When we nourish our body through regular movement and exercise, we feel vibrant and relaxed, with a palpable sense of well-being and a clear mind. The health benefits are innumerable across all the bodies.

Quality sleep is vital to good physical health and affects our alertness, concentration, reaction time, judgment, emotional balance, creativity, clarity, and sense of ease. We still don't understand all that happens during sleep, but we know that it is a dynamic and active process that has an impact on the mind-body-spirit level. When we don't have enough sleep, we can sometimes misinterpret the sense of fatigue as craving for food. You are likely to not be as discerning, and appetite is actually increased. It's easier to reach for high-sugar, carbohydrate, fat, and processed foods for a quick pick-me-up. We have a more positive mood and sense of well-being when we are rested. There are enough challenges in a day without having a deficit of sleep, the resulting poorer mood, and less healthful choices.

Your body needs periods of rest, relaxation, and rejuvenation as well as sleep. It functions optimally with a balance of both doing and being. You may have heard the saying "We are human beings, not human doings!" We have veered toward a contemporary culture that is based on activity and judges a sense of self-worth with achievement. But rest and relaxation are not just for vacation—they are a vital, restorative, and deeply pleasurable part of life. If you don't have enough relaxing and fun activities in your life, you might turn to food to fill that need. The pleasure that food brings, however, is only temporary if you eat too much or eat foods that make you feel unwell on a regular basis.

What We Know

The Right Diet

Everyone is looking for that magic diet or way of eating that promises optimum well-being, health, and weight. As we learn more about food and its interactions with the body, the study of nutrition has evolved from focusing on the basics we need to survive to diets that prevent chronic disease, promote brain health, slow aging, decrease inflammation, benefit gut health, improve moods, and more. We live at a time where the science of nutrition's stretch is wide and exciting but also confusing, with contradictory research popping up now and then.

The full scope of the burgeoning field of nutrition is too vast for this particular book, but the practical model that is presented in this chapter is based on current research on healthy eating. You can use this as a touchstone to evaluate what is right for your body.

There is no one exact diet, no right way of eating for everyone. Our dietary needs at any one time can vary depending upon many factors, including our level of activity, age, stress, health, food sensitivities, genetics, and microbiome.

The mindful eating process offers you a way to eat that brings you fully present to enjoy your food and gain the most nutritionally. How we eat affects how we absorb our food, how much pleasure we get from it, and the quantities we take in. You can deepen your skills in the mindful eating process introduced in chapter 2 by learning to recognize eating triggers and listen to body cues to understand what you really want and need in the moment.

Movement, Sleep, and Relaxation

Movement. Understanding what type of and how much exercise your body needs is also key to your physical nourishment. The American College of Sports Medicine currently recommends 150 minutes of aerobic exercise a week (using the large muscle groups). This on average might look like thirty minutes a day, five days a week.

For weight loss, forty-five minutes to an hour a day is recommended. It doesn't have to be all at the same time, and skipping days too can give the body a break. A gentle, mindful movement practice is also very helpful, as well as finding opportunities to move during your daily activities. (Note: Recommendations do change and guidelines are revised as new research accumulates. Refer to http://www.acsm.org for the most up-to-date advice.)

Sleep. Current recommendations for sleep state that adults should get at least seven hours a night. (School-age children need nine to eleven hours, and teenagers require nine hours on average.) Although most of us can get by with less sleep for a little while, sleep deficits add up quickly and can affect our mood, memory, performance, and the self-care choices we make. When we are not getting enough core sleep, our ability for creative thinking is also affected the next day. Our body produces higher levels of the stress hormone cortisol, which can make us feel irritable and uneasy. Over time excessive cortisol and other factors from inadequate sleep can contribute to chronic health problems.

Some people struggle with ongoing insomnia. It can be helpful to know that with at least 5.5 hours of sleep in a night, research suggests you can maintain your ability for problem solving, alertness, memory, and even reaction time, at least for a little while. But you may not have the full mood and health benefits. The hours beyond minimal "core sleep" are important contributors to enhancing and improving your mood, having a sense of well-being and creativity.

Relaxation. When we have regular periods of rest and relaxation built into our daily lives through leisure activities, creative pursuits, meditation practice, mindful gentle movement, and time spent enjoying nature, we can tangibly measure the positive impact on mental, emotional, and physical health. The parasympathetic nervous system response is switched on, and our heart rate, breathing rate, and blood pressure slow. We might feel warmer, as our body is relaxed and in an optimal state for healing. Without pushing ourselves to get through our to-do list, our brain is in a more creative state. Meditation, for example, disengages the brain from the constant "doing" state and allows us to engage with more parts of our brains, with the possibility of deep healing, integration, and insight.

Practicing relaxation, and engaging in the total-body nourishment practices in this book, builds resilience to stress and provides coping tools and practices that can bring you out of the stress response much sooner. This is crucial if you tend to eat out of stress or boredom and turn to food for pleasure and relief.

Now let's assess and set some intentions for the physical body. You can always adjust your intentions and goals accordingly with the new information and skills introduced.

AWARENESS

○ Pause ○ Reflect ○ Assess

Consider the following questions. (You may recognize some of them from chapter 2; skip any that you've already answered unless your answers have changed.)

~ *Is the way I eat and treat my body now truly nourishing me?*
  Most of the time . . .

~ *Do I eat when I'm hungry and stop when I am comfortably full?*

~ *Do I choose foods and combinations of foods that are healthy, tasty, and leave me feeling energized and satisfied?*

~ *Do I know how to eat in a way that is best for me?*

~ *Do I feed myself high-quality protein, lots of vegetables and fruit, healthy fats, whole grains, legumes and beans, nuts (if you are not allergic), and plenty of water?*

~ *Do I plan ahead so I am not left without food for long periods of time?*

~ *Do I pay attention to what I am eating, savoring the flavors?*

~ *Do I eat regular meals?*

~ *Do I devote regular periods in my schedule to rest and relaxation?*

~ *Do I exercise consistently and/or have a practice of gentle mindful movement such as yoga, qi gong, tai chi, Pilates, or stretching?*

~ Am I being nourished and replenished each night by a good night's sleep?

~ Do I take time out during the day to get up, move around, and stretch?

· ·

~ Do I overeat on a regular basis?

~ Do I eat predominantly to procrastinate, soothe away uncomfortable feelings, ease stress or tension, or because food is there?

~ Do I reach for food to energize me because I am tired?

~ Do I make poorer self-care choices when I am fatigued?

~ Do I often eat while engaging in other activities (e.g., reading, watching TV, cooking) without paying attention to quantity, taste, or satisfaction?

~ Do I often feel spacey or sluggish after meals?

~ Am I fatigued and unfocused during the day?

If you answered yes to most of the first set of questions, and no to the last set, you are probably in very good shape. If you have more noes for the first set and/or any yeses for the last set of questions, you have room to improve your eating and living so that it is truly nourishing you in mind, body, and spirit—most of the time.

Mindful Check-In

What do I notice about the quality of my thoughts, feelings, physical sensations, and sense of well-being after I eat particular foods? After exercising or practicing gentle, mindful movement? After a good night's sleep? What am I aware of in my body, mind, and emotions as I vary the timing of my meals and snacks? What meal timing leaves me feeling most balanced? When do I most commonly engage in the eating behaviors in the reflection questions above? How do these eating behaviors affect me? What am I aware of in my mind, body, and emotions when I am on fast-forward all day and have taken few or no breaks? Consider thoughts, feelings, energy or stress levels, discomfort, pleasant or unpleasant sensations, levels of fatigue, alertness. Shine the light of your awareness before, during, and after eating, exercising, and resting.

INTENTION

What and how would you like your relationship to food to be? What did you notice about how and what you are currently eating affects you? Create an intention for nutrition that would move you closer to a way of eating that would truly nourish you. Take time to write your intention down now in your Well Nourished Journal and/or below.

_____

_____

_____

_____

Create an intention in the area of physical activity that feels authentic and healthy for you. What kind of exercise do you love, and what might bring you joy? Do you like to be outside when you exercise or at a gym? What will be your optimum level of exercise to work toward; at what level can you begin now that feels achievable?

_____

_____

_____

_____

Finally, create intentions for sleep and for rest and relaxation. How would you like your sleep ideally to be? How do the quality and amount of your sleep affect you and keep you nourished? Would you benefit from more rest and relaxation? What kind?

_____

_____

_____

_____

Know Your Eating Triggers

Sometimes our response to eating triggers can take us away from our body's true needs. The triggers themselves are not necessarily bad, but acting upon them mindlessly day after day can add up to a lot of extra food your body doesn't really need. Depending upon your metabolism, your body's unique makeup, your eating choices and habits, you could slowly put on extra weight over time. One study showed that people who ate a meal while playing a computer game reported feeling less full afterward and ate more cookies later than those who ate the same meal but were given a basic mindful eating instruction. This illustrates that those engaged in distracted or mindless eating do not register the full satisfaction or nourishment available from the food and can end up eating more later.

Bringing your awareness to unexpected and habitual eating triggers during the day, including eating paired with distracting activities, provides the opportunity to be mindful at multiple choice points. You can tune in to your hunger, fullness, thoughts, and feelings and see what you really need.

What is your overall intention?

How does this choice in the moment support that?

Are you really hungry?

Discerning that you are not actually hungry, you may simply continue with your activities of the moment. You may consider other options or identify another need in the moment and nourish yourself with that instead. You might want to simply taste the food, sampling a small amount. When you choose to eat, you can do so mindfully, paying attention, savoring, and even celebrating the feast of flavors and senses—from a small amount to a more substantial meal.

Some common eating triggers include:

Seeing Food—in commercials, magazines, store windows, staff-room tables, parties, social events, driving or walking by food businesses, markets, cafés

Smelling Food—cooking in the home, on errands, in malls, at the workplace

Hearing Food—the crunch of your coworkers' chips, the crinkle of a snack bag, the clanking of silverware, the blender making smoothies, the table being set

Social Situations—eating with others, celebrations, meetings, workplace events, restaurant dining

Habitual Activities—pairing food with reading, watching TV, movies, driving, computer use, working, or mindless snacking throughout the day

Stress—eating in response to stressful feelings, thoughts, and situations

Emotional Distress—eating to attempt to soothe away, numb, or avoid difficult feelings: anger, boredom, anxiety, sadness, depression

Procrastinating—eating to avoid tasks, usually bigger tasks or unpleasant tasks

_____ (Other)

List your biggest eating triggers here or in your Well Nourished Journal. Use an additional page as needed:

_____

_____

_____

_____

Mindful Check-In

Mindful eating helps you reconnect with and listen to your body's true signals, as distinct from other eating triggers. With the Mindful Check-In, you will be able to assess your hunger and satiety levels (see page 35 in this chapter) and bring awareness to thoughts, beliefs, and feelings that may affect your choices before and during eating. You can bring self-kindness and compassion to resource the moment rather than distress or judgment.

Practice using an eating trigger as a choice point to check in with what you really need. Use your overall intention and goals to help you make the energizing and nourishing choice that supports your health and lifestyle goals. Even the Mindful Check-In itself can be a source of nourishment, a mindful pause.

Rest in the moment, soaking in and enjoying the peace and clarity of mind that it can offer. In the Mindful Check-In, you may discern you need nourishing activities for the physical body, such as water, food, movement, exercise, relaxation, or healthy pleasures. Or you may discern you need tools and practices for stress-related and emotional eating. (See chapters 5 and 6.)

List of Nourishing Activities

What are all the activities and practices that are nourishing to you? These might include activities that are pleasurable and satisfying in a healthy way. They can apply to any of the bodies, but be sure to include some physical activities to start. Some examples of nourishing activities are:

~ *walking in nature*	~ *taking a hot bath*
~ *having tea with a friend*	~ *dancing*
~ *engaging in a craft or hobby*	~ *receiving a massage*
~ *stretching*	~ *calling a friend*
~ *mindful check-in*	~ *curling up with a book*

Begin your list here and/or in your Well Nourished Journal. Keep it handy as you go through the book. You can call upon your list after your Mindful Check-In. Add new activities as you read through the practices and ideas in each chapter, especially for the bodies you feel could most use nourishment.

_____

_____

_____

_____

How to Face Common Eating Triggers

Habitual Activity Eating. It's not uncommon to have a bag of chips or big plate of leftover pizza disappear when it's sitting next to you and the TV or computer.

Instead of eating while doing something else, if you are hungry, try having a snack before and eating it mindfully, savoring it with all your senses. With or without an activity, deciding on a portion size before you engage is helpful rather than sitting down with the entire box or bag. Then bring awareness to the snack when you do eat, shifting your attention to the act of eating. Try staying connected to your body's signals of hunger, pleasure, and fullness. Adjust your portion size accordingly so you can feel good, not stuffed or full with food you didn't need or want in the first place.

Silent Meal

Try making one meal or snack a day a silent, mindful one, to practice and deepen your foundational mindful eating practice. Eat without engaging in any other activities. Even if you only practice for a short amount of time during a meal, it will help you bring this awareness to eating in other situations over the day and create a positive habit.

Procrastination. Many people fritter away the day focusing on all the little, easily doable activities before taking on the bigger projects. Once smaller tasks are completed, you may feel a momentary sense of satisfaction as you cross them off your list. And many people use food to procrastinate doing tasks big or small, or to distract themselves.

Yet however you put things off, underlying worry can grow as the bigger, more important task remains incomplete over the day, weeks, even months. Learning skills to prevent procrastination can decrease the sense of worry and anxiety from procrastinating itself. It can help ease the stress that leads to eating.

You might try starting with your biggest project first instead. Break it down into small, manageable steps. Determine how much time you are willing to spend on it; when that time is up, soak in the sense of accomplishment from what you've done. Acknowledge and reward yourself with appreciation, gratitude, and maybe a nourishing activity.

You will find tools to address other common eating triggers and challenges, such as social situations, stress, and emotional eating, in the following chapters.

Tips for Managing Eating Triggers

1. *Read through the list of eating triggers and see if any seem familiar to you.*

2. *Make a list of any eating triggers that you can't fully control or would like to better master.*

3. *Practice the Mindful Check-In to discern what you really need when these eating triggers arise.*

4. *Use the variety of skills and tools throughout the book as is helpful.*

5. *Start a List of Nourishing Activities for each body (see above). You can add to it as you go through the book. Choose when to engage in a nourishing activity instead of eating.*

A Healthy Diet for Your Body

Whole-Foods, Plant-Based Nutrition. In research and population studies several dietary patterns seem to be the healthiest for overall well-being, longevity, and chronic disease prevention. A plant-based, whole-foods diet appears to be the winner. A plant-based diet can include small amounts of animal products (such as fish, chicken, and/or red meat), but the fewer of these the greater the health benefit. The more plant protein in a diet, the lower the risk of many diseases. The so-called Mediterranean diet, which includes vegetables, fruits, nuts, legumes, whole grains, olive oil, and fish is the best known. This is not a specific diet but a way of eating that has been found to deliver great health benefits.

Whole-foods, plant-based nutrition is healthiest for us and our environment (current large-scale livestock practices significantly contribute to global warming), helps prevent and sometimes reverse disease, and contributes to longevity. It provides us with a wide variety of vitamins, minerals, antioxidants, phytochemicals, fiber, protein, and healthy fats that we need for optimum health. It is good for our heart and brain, cancer prevention, diabetes prevention and management, weight, and overall health. It helps keep blood sugar even, improves our moods and feelings of well-being, and reduces cravings.

Some people do better with more animal protein; others benefit from more or less carbohydrates for optimum health. Mindful eating can help you discern the right balance for your body, which can change over a life span with childhood, adolescence, pregnancy, lactation, sports training, acute or chronic disease, and aging.

Sometimes Foods. Regardless of the proportion or types of foods being promoted, there is one food group that all nutrition experts agree is not essential—empty calories, discretionary calories, or highly palatable foods. These are the foods that offer calories for quick energy but virtually no nutritional benefits. They are the high-fat, high-sugar, high-salt foods made with refined carbohydrates that have had all the nutrition stripped out of them. They may give your taste buds a jolt at first and your insulin a ride. Food companies spend a lot of time engineering these "highly palatable" snacks. Fortunately, when we really tune in to the pleasure of the taste, we often find it decreases after a few bites.

Applying the principles and tools of mindful eating can help you if you wish to include these foods on occasion, but in small quantities—feeling in control, enjoying the taste, and letting go of feeling guilty or bad. Everything in moderation, as they say.

Mindful Inquiry Food Log

Whatever way of eating you choose, know the research but also know your own body. Find a way of eating in alignment with your body by mindfully tuning in throughout the day. How do your body, mind, and spirit feel before, during, and after eating particular foods and meals? What is your energy like, your alertness, your feeling of well-being? When do you feel best and most in balance? Adjust and fine-tune what works best for you.

To begin this inquiry keep a Mindful Inquiry Food Log for three days in your Well Nourished Journal. Fill in one row for each meal or snack.

MINDFUL INQUIRY FOOD LOG

Day:

Time:	Mindful Check-In Before: *(Thoughts/ Feelings/Energy)*	Type of Food:	Type of Drink:	Mindful Check-In During and After: *(Thoughts/ Feelings/Energy)*
○ Meal *or* ○ Snack		Amount:	Amount:	
Other Observations:				
Time:	Mindful Check-In Before: *(Thoughts/ Feelings/Energy)*	Type of Food:	Type of Drink:	Mindful Check-In During and After: *(Thoughts/ Feelings/Energy)*
○ Meal *or* ○ Snack		Amount:	Amount:	
Other Observations:				
Time:	Mindful Check-In Before: *(Thoughts/ Feelings/Energy)*	Type of Food:	Type of Drink:	Mindful Check-In During and After: *(Thoughts/ Feelings/Energy)*
○ Meal *or* ○ Snack		Amount:	Amount:	
Other Observations:				
Time:	Mindful Check-In Before: *(Thoughts/ Feelings/Energy)*	Type of Food:	Type of Drink:	Mindful Check-In During and After: *(Thoughts/ Feelings/Energy)*
○ Meal *or* ○ Snack		Amount:	Amount:	
Other Observations:				
Time:	Mindful Check-In Before: *(Thoughts/ Feelings/Energy)*	Type of Food:	Type of Drink:	Mindful Check-In During and After: *(Thoughts/ Feelings/Energy)*
○ Meal *or* ○ Snack		Amount:	Amount:	
Other Observations:				
Time:	Mindful Check-In Before: *(Thoughts/ Feelings/Energy)*	Type of Food:	Type of Drink:	Mindful Check-In During and After: *(Thoughts/ Feelings/Energy)*
○ Meal *or* ○ Snack		Amount:	Amount:	
Other Observations:				

The Well Nourished Plate

Just as it is helpful for chefs to know the basics of their craft before creating their delicious dishes, it is helpful to know the basics of a healthy way of eating. Our user-friendly, flexible eating and nutrition model, the Well Nourished Plate, is based on the best of current research, using a format similar to the USDA My Plate. From here you can adjust and find what works best for your body. Be flexible, embellish, get creative, and find the proportions and types of foods that you love and that work for your unique body—a way of eating that supports you to feel healthy and vibrant.

Basic guidelines for a healthy plate include increasing vegetables, fruits, beans, lentils, whole grains, seeds, and nuts in your diet; decreasing saturated fat, which comes mainly from animal products; and limiting processed and highly refined foods (such as candy, cookies, and cake).

The plate method is a useful way of conceptualizing your meals to get a good balance of types of foods and nutrients over a day. We can use it simply as a guide to think about the proportions and amounts of food from each group as we plan our meals, and tune in to what we want and need.

Having a visual guide helps us increase the amounts of vegetables and fruits we eat, while having a moderate amount of carbohydrates and proteins. In the typical Western diet we tend to eat more protein than we need. Since vegetables and fruits are often the least consumed in the Western diet, look for creative ways to incorporate more of them in your meals and snacks throughout the day. Experiment with the amount of carbohydrates that feels optimum to your body at a meal or over the day. Perhaps you may have less than a quarter plate and increase vegetables and fruits.

Using these very basic mindful nutrition guidelines, you can enjoy healthy meals and snacks. Include your favorite foods that will delight your palate and tummy.

YOUR WELL NOURISHED PLATE... SIMPLY A GUIDE

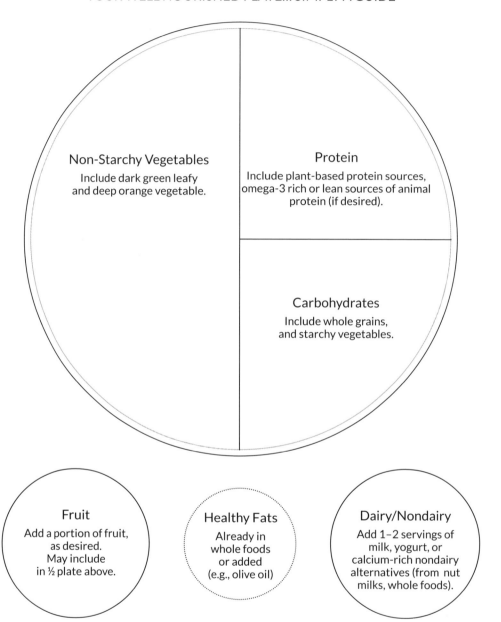

Non-Starchy Vegetables
Include dark green leafy
and deep orange vegetable.

Protein
Include plant-based protein sources,
omega-3 rich or lean sources of animal
protein (if desired).

Carbohydrates
Include whole grains,
and starchy vegetables.

Fruit
Add a portion of fruit,
as desired.
May include
in ½ plate above.

Healthy Fats
Already in
whole foods
or added
(e.g., olive oil)

Dairy/Nondairy
Add 1–2 servings of
milk, yogurt, or
calcium-rich nondairy
alternatives (from nut
milks, whole foods).

Eat a rainbow of colors in your diet.

On your plate aim for:

~ *One-half vegetables; also fruit if desired*

~ *One-quarter protein; legumes, beans, nuts, seeds, tofu, fish, poultry, reduced or no red meat (depending on mindful exploration of your body)*

~ *One-quarter carbohydrates, such as whole grains*

~ *A small to moderate amount of healthy fats already in whole foods or added (olives, avocados, nuts, seeds, salmon, eggs, flaxseed, olive or organic canola oil)*

~ *Plenty of water*

Consider these possibilities:		
Vegetables and Fruit	**Protein**	**Carbohydrate (Whole Food)**
~ Dark leafy greens, deep orange–colored vegetables, cruciferous vegetables, green salads (with a variety of vegetables)	~ Lean chicken, fish (Include omega-3 rich choices such as salmon, trout and herring), lean turkey	~ Whole grains (which retain the fiber, vitamins, and minerals and other important nutrients)
~ Stir-fried or steamed veggies	~ If you include red meat, limit or avoid processed meat. Choose lean cuts and grass-fed sources (which have a higher concentration of healthy omega-3's).	~ Brown rice, quinoa, rolled oats, whole grain and high-fiber breads, pasta, corn, cereal
~ Smoothies with a large handful of greens		~ Starchy vegetables, such as fresh peas, corn, potatoes, sweet potatoes, yams
~ Vegetable sticks for snacks (add hummus or peanut butter for protein and healthy fat)	~ Legumes, beans, tofu, walnuts, almonds, cashews, other nuts, nut butters, cheeses, eggs	
~ One to three servings of fruit a day—the deeper colored the fruit, the more health-promoting nutrition		

Gluten Sensitivity

Many people wonder if they are gluten sensitive or intolerant. The percentage of those that are truly gluten intolerant with celiac disease is small, although rising. If you suspect you may be intolerant it's important to get tested by a doctor or naturopath. For sensitivity, you may try eliminating gluten from your diet to see if it makes a difference in how you feel. Many people report that a variety of symptoms subside when they go gluten free. Choosing organic grains may make a difference too.

Meal Timing and Planning

The body tends to do best with eating at regular intervals throughout the day, so it gets consistent amounts of high-quality fuel. When you have a meal or snack that has balanced amounts of protein, healthy fats, and healthy carbohydrates, you give your body various sources of energy and nutrients that break down and digest at different intervals, resulting in an even release of energy over time. If you skip meals or don't honor hunger at those in-between times, you may find yourself with lower energy, less focus, irritability, and uneven mood. Three meals a day is the standard for most people with a snack or two in between. Some people do better with more frequent, smaller meals throughout the day. Research in this area indicates that those who eat less than three meals a day actually tend to be more overweight.

Listen to your body and find the meal and snack timing that works for you—to help you feel the best, with good energy, focus, and mood. Practice bringing awareness to environmental triggers, making mindful choices and eating your meals mindfully to support you.

Try planning ahead so that you can have delicious and healthful meals and snacks throughout the day. Depending upon the day or week, that includes planning for grocery shopping; leaving time for preparing, cooking, and eating meals; or knowing where you can buy a healthy meal or snack within your time constraints, financial resources, or location.

Deepen Your Mindful Eating

Mindful eating includes paying attention to the entire process of eating without judgment or blame, eliciting gratitude and appreciation for what you are eating, recognizing the interconnectedness of the food you eat with nature, the people involved, the elements of the earth, and finally tuning in mindfully to the interaction of the food with you and your body. Awareness of thoughts, beliefs, feelings, and environment can help guide your choices. When you are fully engaged while eating, the mind becomes quiet and the eating experience is pure nourishment and delight.

Let's take a closer look at some of the aspects of the seven tips to mindful eating that were introduced in chapter 2.

Seven Tips to Mindful Eating

1. *Do a Mindful Check-In.*
2. *Check in with your hunger and fullness level before eating.*
3. *Gaze, reflect, and appreciate.*
4. *Enjoy eating with all your senses.*
5. *Taste mindfully.*
6. *Check in with hunger and fullness while eating.*
7. *Practice.*

Mindful Check-In. If you are feeling tense or uncentered before eating, begin with a few deep, relaxing breaths. Then let your breath return to a natural pace. With a gentle focus on the breath, allow your awareness to expand outward to include your whole body and mind. Notice any thoughts or feelings that are present. How might these inform your experience right now? Is there a desire to eat out of a tense thought or difficult emotion? What happens if you intend to let go of that thought or feeling with a deep inhale and an extended exhale? Perhaps you've created a space where you can tune in to what you really need, food or otherwise.

Gaze, Reflect, Appreciate. Reflecting on how the food got to you and what went into making it helps you feel connected to and appreciate the elements and people involved. This is a great antidote to mindless eating. If you tend to eat mindlessly or have anxious thoughts about food before eating, simply bring in a moment or so of gratitude to shift your state and allow the corresponding positive brain and body neurochemicals to flow. Focus your thoughts on how fortunate you are to have this snack or meal before you. Gratitude elicits more positive emotions, such as joy, optimism, and happiness, and helps you feel less lonely and isolated. When you eat with appreciation and joy, you may find to your surprise that you need less to feel satisfied.

Taste Mindfully. Paying attention to taste gives us the opportunity to savor our food and derive great pleasure and satisfaction from it, and to choose to stop eating when it stops being tasty. Our taste buds tire, as all of our senses do eventually, when bombarded by stimuli. Fortunately for us, they seem to tire most rapidly when we eat highly processed foods, high in refined carbohydrates, salt, sugar, fat, and other fillers. Eating a complex meal, with a variety of healthy foods, is an enjoyable process and keeps your taste buds active. But once you've had enough, food often just doesn't taste as good. We can use awareness of taste both to fully enjoy our food and also to be more discriminating about what and how much we eat.

Do I Supplement?

Sometimes you may need supplementation, depending upon your own body's health and nutrition needs or digestive limitations. Guidance from a mindfulness-based registered dietitian nutritionist or other highly trained nutritionist may be helpful in these cases. If you suspect you may have some nutritional deficiencies, you might get tested for levels of specific vitamins or minerals and give a diet and health history. Recommended evidence-based supplementation might include omega-3 fatty acids, vitamin D, calcium, vitamin B12, folic acid, iron, or probiotics, among others.

Hunger Awareness. Hunger occurs when you have used up most of your stores of readily available energy from your last meal or snack and your blood sugar level drops. If you don't eat at the first signs of hunger, it will slowly increase. If it gets too high, you tend to eat whatever is available, losing the discrimination and natural ability to choose that you have at lower levels of hunger. You enjoy your food more when you have some hunger, and you feed your body fuel that you really need. When you are very hungry, your body is primed to get energy and nutrition fast, overriding your executive functioning and your rational mind. You become so focused on getting food fast, your body tries to make up for the missing energy with food thoughts, feelings, physical sensations, and finally behaviors. This is what can happen when you skip meals, go on diets, and restrict calories to an unnaturally low level. Eventually the body's biological drive to make up for calories and the psychological sense of deprivation can lead to imbalances and overeating.

HUNGER AWARENESS SCALE

1	2	3	4	5	6	7	8	9	10
not hungry				moderately hungry					starving

Check in with your body, particularly the stomach area, noticing how hungry you are. Once you've found your hunger experience, give it a number on the scale, with 1 being not hungry at all and 10 being the most starving you can imagine. Then pause and tune in to the specific body sensations that help you identify it. Practice at varying times during the day to get to know your body's signals at different levels.

When you know your hunger experience at different levels, you can more easily check in with your hunger at various times of the day. Most people feel fine at low levels on the hunger scale. As you move up the scale, hunger "pangs" and other sensations may emerge and increase in intensity. Some people may not experience hunger in the stomach at first, just an achiness in the head, irritability, anger, a sense of panic or spaciness. Tuning in to hunger and your body's signals will grow your awareness and get easier with time. You'll be able to recognize whether a desire or cue to eat is from physical hunger, emotional hunger, or sometimes both. This will help you decide why, how, and what you want to feed your body when you ask yourself, Am I physically hungry? What do I really need right now?

Fullness Awareness. What is being full and satisfied? There are several ways to know when you have had enough. While hunger subsides as you meet your energy requirements, actual physical fullness, the sensation you experience from the distention of the stomach, increases with the volume of food or liquid in your belly. Fullness experience on the 10-point scale can range from the low end, with no sensation or feelings of emptiness, to stuffed, bloated, uncomfortable, tired, sluggish, or lethargic on the high end. People usually report a level of comfortable fullness around 6, where you can walk and move easily and carry on with the activities of your day. You may feel satisfied, energized, and still alert.

When you tune in to both hunger and fullness, you can notice when you feel satisfied without always having a corresponding level of physical fullness. You might eat a small amount of rich food that may completely satisfy your hunger yet doesn't produce a proportional feeling of physical fullness. You could eat too much of a rich food if fullness has been your only signal to stop eating. Conversely, you can eat a large quantity of a low-calorie food, such as celery sticks or air-popped popcorn, and feel physically full without meeting your energy and nutrient needs. Don't let this fool you as your fullness subsides. If you are not tuned in to your hunger level as it increases and you don't honor it before it gets very uncomfortable, you may end up overeating.

FULLNESS AWARENESS SCALE

1	2	3	4	5	6	7	8	9	10
not full				comfortably full					most full

Check in with your body, noticing how full you are. Pay attention to sensations and experiences in your stomach. Once you've found your fullness experience, give it a number on a scale from 1 to 10, with 1 being not full at all and 10 being the most full (e.g., after a holiday dinner). Once you've found your fullness level, pause and tune in to whatever helps you identify your fullness level.

People report experiencing low levels of fullness as empty or neutral. As the fullness scale increases, you might experience growing pressure, bloating, and finally outright discomfort from being overstuffed.

It is helpful to have awareness of both hunger and fullness levels. Experiment with these inquiries. Bring awareness to your hunger levels for a few days or a few weeks first and then practice awareness of fullness. Get to know how your body responds at different levels by tuning in at various times of the day. Notice what levels feel good for your body, mind, and brain.

Common Hunger Patterns

One common hunger pattern is to skip breakfast, have a light to medium-size lunch, and then feel starved by the time dinner rolls around. You might snack through dinner preparation, eat a larger than comfortable dinner, and perhaps even snack through the evening.

Or maybe you have eaten a satisfying breakfast and lunch. At 3:30 or 4:00 p.m. you feel hungry but override those signals with thoughts such as "I shouldn't be eating now," "I'm going to push through this," "I will have dinner in a few hours," "I'm trying to lose weight," or _____ (fill in the blank). When dinnertime comes, you may follow the same dinner and evening pattern as above, although to a lesser degree, because you overrode your hunger cues in the late afternoon.

Maybe you're not even conscious of signs of hunger throughout the day. This can lead to skipping meals, forgetting to eat, and then suddenly being aware of a strong level of hunger at an 8 or 9 on the scale. At that point it's more difficult to make healthy choices and eat to comfortably full, which could lead to overeating later in the day.

You might never let yourself feel hungry, eating throughout the day. This pattern is sometimes established after a childhood when food was scarce and the next substantial meal time was dubious. If this is familiar, you might ask yourself, Is this working for me? Are you enjoying your food as much as you could if you let yourself actually get a little hungry before your next meal? Are you eating more than you need (and maybe slowly gaining weight) because you are not attuned to your true hunger?

Think about your relationship to hunger and any patterns you notice. Are you in tune with your body's hunger signals and do you eat in a way that honors them? Do you feel in control of the amount you eat? What would it be like to make more conscious choices about hunger?

Mindful Satiety

An overall sense of satiety arises as you digest a good meal or snack, letting you know you've had enough. Your sense of well-being will depend upon the quality of food and nutritional input and how your body responds to the food. It can be more subtle at first and doesn't come as quickly as the feedback from the other awarenesses. But it can be a powerful indicator of how your body responds to food, depending upon quality, freshness, source, meal time, and amounts. What you notice from mindful satiety can guide you in future meal choices, timing, and planning.

Choose to Move

Do you turn to food or other ways to "nourish" yourself that are not helpful when you don't feel good physically in your body from lack of exercise or stress buildup? There are countless benefits of exercise to your well-being, for your mind, body, and spirit. These include improved memory, better mood, greater confidence and better self-image, and all-around more positive outlook. Exercise also helps with weight management, a stronger heart and cardiovascular system, and lower blood pressure.

If you practice mindfully, not forcing or exerting too much effort, exercise can be a pleasant, stress-reducing experience. If your mind tends to run away while you exercise, gently bring it back to the breath and to the felt sensation of movement in the body. You can get a vacation from the mind and consciously choose where you want your thoughts to go.

Before beginning an exercise program, it's always a good idea to talk with your doctor if you have preexisting health conditions or have been sedentary for over three months. Check out the American College of Sports Medicine's more specific guidelines (http://www.acsm.org).

Enhance Your Sleep

Sleep tips, often called sleep hygiene, offer behavioral and environmental approaches that help make a difference in how much and how well you sleep. Mindfulness practices powerfully enhance the effectiveness. Try these suggestions if you need better sleep. Pick a few to experiment with to see what is true for you. Most important, notice what time you naturally want to fall asleep. Are you keeping yourself up with screen time (computer work, Internet surfing, TV)? Does your bedtime really work for you?

Sleep Tips

~ *Expose yourself to the morning sunlight upon awakening.*

~ *When you can't fall asleep, practice mindfulness meditation or a relaxing body scan (focus on your breathing, then gently, mindfully bring kind and nourishing attention to each part of your body, starting from the feet, slowly moving up to the head, simply noticing any sensations that are present without judgment), or personal prayer. Use the time for reverie and relaxation.*

~ *Practice eliciting positive emotions such as joy, gratitude, and kindness.*

~ *Avoid heavy meals and eat at least three hours before bedtime.*

Replenish with Mindfulness Meditation and Relaxation Practices

Mindfulness meditation not only cultivates mindful awareness and helps you learn to respond rather than react to your experiences; it also elicits the relaxation response while you are practicing. As you meditate, you might be aware of scattered thoughts and some agitation in your mind but at the same time be aware that your body is calmer and more peaceful. By not reacting or engaging with the thoughts, you eventually touch a quieter practice, permeated with calm and peace.

Bringing a mindful pause to the moments of your day with breath awareness or a few intentional deeper breaths can also help still any agitation in the mind and prevent further spiraling out. A mindful pause can offer some relaxation, or a return to baseline, with the important benefit of clearer thoughts, feelings, and emotions. It's easier to make nourishing choices for yourself from this place.

The body responds positively to relaxation and healthy pleasures with a host of beneficial changes akin to the parasympathetic response and more. Schedule any of the following activities daily, weekly, or monthly. Regardless, when you engage in them, be very present and bring your mind back when your attention wanders away. Choose a mindful walking practice (particularly in nature), mindfulness-based yoga, qi gong, or tai chi. Hot showers or baths with your favorite soaps and shampoos scented with essential oils can also relax your body and mind. You could even indulge in a massage, pedicure, hot tub, facial, or other treatment at least once a month as your budget allows. Spend time unwinding by reading, engaging in hobbies, or talking with friends, and commit to nourishing conversation that supports and uplifts rather than focusing on what's not working (sharing challenges and offering mutual support and wisdom with a positive focus can be nourishing too).

Inspire a Meal with Beauty

When you prepare a meal, enhance the experience by choosing a beautiful environment in which to enjoy it. It could be a picnic in the countryside or on a bench by a fountain in a park. At home create soft lighting with candles, put out flowers and nice placemats, or use plates that make you smile. Perhaps play relaxing background music. Take your time eating the meal, savoring with all your senses, and pay attention to when you are comfortably satisfied. More elements than just the food will nourish you with this meal.

OUTER SUPPORT

We have reviewed many skills and tools to help us meet our nutritional needs and enhance our eating with mindfulness. The eating trigger guidelines are a good first start and may be something you can explore with a check-in buddy. Experiment with the Healthy Plate model, finding food amounts and choices that feel right for your body. Keep a Mindful Eating Inquiry Log for a few days. Try cooking new foods or going to a restaurant with healthy cuisine from other cultures, which is a fun way to share with others. Clean out foods from the pantry you no longer use or want, donate them to a food bank, and make room for new foods. Check out the local farmers' market. With each visit, try some new vegetables to incorporate into meals and snacks. Buy a new cookbook to get inspired. Invite a buddy to eat one meal or snack mindfully with you.

To fully support your exercise goals and routine, you might ask a buddy to exercise with you on some days. Set a date and time so you won't be tempted to skip it. You could also get into a regular routine of walking your dog. Slowly lengthen the amount of time or frequency of your exercise. Join a gym, walking club, hiking group, rowing club—being with a group of friends or like-minded exercisers will be motivating and stimulating. Buy new exercise clothes, gym shoes, yoga mats, whatever you need to support your new habits. Decide weekly or at the beginning of each day when you are going to exercise—scheduling can be key to sticking with your routine. Finally, consider creating a calendar of your favorite yoga or other exercise classes. Post it over your desk so you can look every day to see which classes will fit into your schedule, or make your schedule around them.

If you regularly sleep in the same room with someone at night or have house-mates, let them know your needs in terms of lights-out, bedtime hour, and noise levels. Play some white noise or gentle, soft music in your room to help you relax and fall asleep.

For mindfulness and relaxation support, participate in a weekly or monthly local meditation group, join a program that offers online interactive meditation sessions, deepen your practice with a meditation retreat, and/or use apps, recordings, webinars, and videos to support your practice.

INNER RESOURCES

Practice eating at least one meal or snack mindfully each day. Try mastering the building blocks of mindful eating awareness one or two at time (hunger, fullness, taste), following the order they are presented. Add another when you feel some comfort or proficiency. Practice until it becomes an effortless, conscious habit to pay attention and eat in this way.

If you find you are resistant to a planned exercise or movement session, consider all the reasons why it would be so beneficial for you—physically, mentally, spiritually. Think about how you will feel better and have more energy, less tension in the body, less stress, and less stress eating. Consider your options for classes or routines and what will work best for you.

Do an occasional Mindful Check-In to see what you really need during the day and give that to yourself even if it is just a quick stretch or walk. It's so easy to keep doing the work projects, going down the list of errands, ignoring the body's need for movement or a break, to feel good and balanced. It may even be easier to grab something to eat to distract yourself, procrastinate, or to try to feel better, when you really just need to move and are not even hungry. Engage in regular nourishing and relaxing activities to keep yourself resourced and resilient.

Don't forget to practice self-compassion and caring. Research shows that when we are more caring toward ourselves, we are more apt to engage in healthy behaviors.

Your SPRIGS Goals

Fine-tune your intentions in all the areas we've discussed to specific, doable actions using SPRIGS. Revisit these at least every few weeks.

Create your specific SPRIGS for nutrition and mindful eating, as well as for exercise, sleep, and relaxation. Write them down here or in your Well Nourished Journal. Make each of them into goals that are specific, positive, realistic, inspiring, and grounded in time. Finally, gauge your goal and set your next steps.

Use Your 5 Steps Prompter Tools

[ ] Fill in the physical body in your Well Nourished Bowl.

[ ] Fill out your Intention and Goals Prompter for the physical body (include nutrition and mindful eating, exercise, and sleep and relaxation).

[ ] Use your 5 Steps Daily Prompter to help support you in mindful choices.

CHAPTER FIVE

Emotional Nourishment: Cultivating Balance and Self-Compassion

Mindfulness practice teaches us how to meet and greet emotions with a nonjudgmental mind and a nourishing kind awareness.

Emotions can be likened to the weather: always changing to some degree. They arise in response to events happening around us, to our thoughts and internal states. They are impacted by how we are tending to our whole life and taking care of our physical body. Our emotions, particularly the challenging ones, may be signals that something needs attention on our journey of life. They also may be responses to a variety of random thoughts that arise and pass away throughout the day. It's easy to get stuck in the emotion of the moment, let it color our full experience, and react from inside that feeling. When we learn to navigate difficult emotions mindfully, we can find a place of balance and ease. Feelings of peace and joy might actually increase.

Having a well-watered ground of physical nourishment is so important to a re-sourced emotional body. In the last chapter we looked at how essential healthy nutri-tion, sleep, exercise, and relaxation are to the body. All of these affect the health of our emotional body. Eating well and at regular intervals contributes to an overall sense of well-being and energy. Sufficient sleep provides mood-enhancing benefits, while not enough sleep can make us irritable and contribute to depression. Regular movement and exercise increase positive mood and optimism and help stave off depression. Mindfulness practices with their relaxation side effect can particularly help your emo-tional well-being. Overall, with good physical nourishment you have more resiliency and body resources to draw upon when the inevitable curves of life come your way.

What We Know

It's perfectly human to have emotions. They may drive us to create great art, engage in meaningful work, or be a wonderful friend and contributor to our community. The passion from anger, love, or concern may compel us to do great things to make a dif-ference in the world and in other people's lives.

But challenging emotions can blindside us, overtake us, immobilize us, or simply make us feel uneasy. These, along with unmanaged stress, can affect our health and well-being. The tools and practices in this chapter have been shown to improve emo-tional balance by reducing challenging emotional states and increasing positive emo-tions. Learning to accept emotions mindfully, paradoxically, helps bring more peace and balance. For example, at least one study indicates that practicing self-compassion is linked to decreased depression and anxiety and increased well-being. When people are happier and more self-compassionate, they make healthier choices for themselves in their lives.

Now take a few moments to reflect, assess, and set an intention in this area.

AWARENESS

○ Pause ○ Reflect ○ Assess

Ask yourself the following questions.

~ *Do I have ways to nourish myself and come to back to balance when I have strong emotions?*

~ *Do I have the skills and tools I need to make nurturing choices for myself when I am upset?*

~ *When I am upset, do I check in and give myself what I really need most of the time?*

~ *Do I engage in fun and pleasurable activities on a regular basis?*

~ *Do I tend to push away, distract, or overindulge in feelings?*

~ *When I am feeling upset or bored, do I soothe or numb feelings with food or other activities?*

~ *When I feel strong difficult emotions, do I judge myself and often think I should be feeling a different way?*

If any of the first four statements ring true for you most of the time, you have some good practices already in place. If any of the last four statements are true for you, learning ways to nurture the emotional body will be very helpful.

Mindful Check-In

Next time you are upset, take a few breaths and note thoughts, feelings, and bodily sensations. What happens? Watch your usual resulting choices and actions. Are these helpful and healthy choices in the short term? In the long term? What do you really need in that moment to ease your distress?

INTENTION

Create an intention based on your assessment to increase nourishment of your emotional body. Write it down here and/or in your Well Nourished Journal.

_____

_____

_____

_____

We are all connected, and like it or not, even if we aren't consciously aware of it, what happens in another part of the planet affects us. How do we manage the helplessness we feel when we turn on the evening news or read about another environmental or human catastrophe in the world or our community? We might feel it directly and have it spill over into our relationships with those close to us. We might drown some of the discomfort in food, alcohol, or excessive television watching or screen surfing. How do we navigate all these changing inner and outer circumstances with love, grace, ease, and compassion?

We can elicit positive emotions that will nourish us, our physiology, our hearts, our minds, and our spirits. Positive emotions—which we experience when we help, connect and bond, and share with others—facilitate our survival. Negative emotions arise when we feel our survival is threatened in some way and indicate an action may be called for. (In chapter 6 we will explore how to navigate thoughts that elicit emotions.) Sometimes we may need to take very real actions, but we can do so from a resourced place.

Are you quick to judge your experience, thinking you should be feeling a different way than you actually are? When you shine the light of your awareness on emotions, you will see that there is usually a subtle or not-so-subtle resistance to uncomfortable feelings. It might manifest in the body as tension or frustration. You might even have an emotion about the emotion you are feeling (e.g., fear of an emotion's intensity, anger at yourself for feeling envy of another), not accepting what is actually true for you in the moment, which can lead to more stress, more judgment, and more uncomfortable feelings or intensity. To numb the discomfort, some people turn to food or overeat. What if you meet and greet the initial uncomfortable feeling with mindfulness? Through practicing sitting meditation, a Mindful Check-In, and mindfulness of daily activities, you build your capacity to face an uncomfortable feeling with a calm and steady attention that defuses it or at least makes it more tolerable. This helps counter the habitual impulses to shut a feeling down by ignoring it, pushing it away, or engaging in a numbing activity.

In fact, we can meet our experience with a nourishing, kind, and compassionate awareness. How wonderful to be able to rest more peacefully in the moment even if sadness or anger is passing through us. By tempering the potentially overwhelming intensity of an emotion, we can clearly see what we need. We learn that we are not that emotion, but that it is simply part of our experience temporarily, just passing through.

It's natural to feel upset when we see injustices in the world and to our blue-green planet. If we open to this feeling without pushing it away, it may lead us to more action to right things in the world, even if it begins with our own community. When you experience a personal loss or challenging circumstance in your life, gather and activate your resources. Nourish yourself with kind and compassionate attention, love, friends, community, support, all the ways you can nourish yourself. Celebrate being human—that you are alive and can feel the myriad emotions that are part of your humanness.

Positive emotions directly counteract the negative emotions we feel when we are triggered by something or are under stress. You can cultivate balance and self-compassion with the following practices. You can work with specific mindfulness practices to help ease pain and discomfort and open the heart instead of the mouth. First let's reframe how we look at emotions: They are a part of being human; they are not wrong and they are not bad. One of the biggest takeaways mindfulness practice can offer us is how to meet and greet emotions with a nonjudgmental mind, even with kindness.

SKILLS AND TOOLS

Elicit Positive Emotions and Qualities

When you practice mindfulness meditation, there are moments when you begin to experience your mind as pure spacious awareness. Nonjudgment and acceptance help lead the way. This awareness of the true nature of your mind begins to grow and becomes a part of your understanding of who you are—more than your passing feelings, emotions, thoughts, what happens to you, and how you respond to these inner and outer experiences. You are a vast reservoir of peace and calm that is disturbed only by the fluctuations of the mind and your response to the naturally changing circumstances of life. This awareness helps to bring a sense of perspective in the challenging moments. When we dwell in this awareness, positive emotions naturally arise, such as peace, joy, calm, a lightness of being, tranquility. They are part of this essential mind and signal that everything is all right. We feel fully fed. We can learn to dwell more in and identify with spacious mind through mindfulness meditation practice and other methods. Let's take a look at what some of these practices are that help connect us to our essential self.

Mindfulness of Breath Practice

1. Find a comfortable place to sit, close your eyes, or keep eyes open with a soft downward gaze. Sit upright with hands folded or resting on your lap.
2. Begin your sitting meditation practice by focusing your attention on the breath. Be curious about the texture, sensation, and duration of the breath.
3. Notice when your attention has wandered and meet each new object of attention with kindness and without judgment. Then return your attention to the breath.
4. As the mind becomes quieter, rest in and enjoy the peace and spaciousness that emerge in your natural awareness. As new objects of attention arise in your awareness, repeat this process.

Practice for ten to forty-five minutes (or longer if desired).

Spacious Mind Practice

Begin your sitting meditation practice, as you did for mindfulness of breath practice, by focusing your attention on the breath. Halfway through your practice period, let go of the breath as your main focus of attention. Simply rest in pure awareness of whatever is present. Allow thoughts, feelings, sounds, and physical sensations to come to you, rather than looking for them. When you become aware of them, do not push them away, resist, or judge them. Embrace them with your welcoming attention whether they are pleasant or unpleasant, without engaging in any thought stories or reactions. Watch as they arise and pass away in the field of your attention. Practice for twenty to forty-five minutes.

Lovingkindness practice is a sister practice to mindfulness practice. We intentionally cultivate the quality of lovingkindness by repeating nourishing phrases to ourselves and to others, a practice of well-wishing. This helps soften and open the heart of kindness. Negative emotions can slowly begin to melt away. Over time, as with all practices, it gets easier. You can tap into the quality of lovingkindness more easily and lead with an attitude of kindness in your life. This is nourishing medicine to your own cells as well as to others.

Lovingkindness Practice

1. Begin your sitting meditation practice, as you did for the others, by focusing your attention on the breath.

2. About ten to fifteen minutes into the practice, begin to shift your attention to the center of your chest. Breathe in and out as though you are filling your heart with this nourishing breath.

3. Begin to imagine the quality of warmth and lovingkindness filling your heart in whatever way is comfortable for you. You might bring to mind people or pets you really care about, or warm and loving memories of family and friends. You might imagine a lotus flower opening in the center of your heart, petals unfolding, spreading love and kindness throughout your body.

4. When you feel a shift, perhaps an opening or softening of your heart center or a sense of ease in the body, mind, or heart, begin to repeat phrases of well-wishing, of lovingkindness to yourself. These might include:

~ *May I be healthy and happy.*

~ *May I be peaceful and at ease.*

~ *May my heart be filled with lovingkindness.*

You may also add some of your own if you wish.

5. Repeat and offer these phrases to yourself several times. Then send them to someone you care about, someone beloved to you. This could be a person or a pet. For the full traditional practice, offer these phrases in the following order:

1. to yourself

2. to someone you care about

3. to a neutral person

4. to a challenging person (but not the most challenging)

5. finally to all living beings in the world

6. As you move through the order of recipients, substitute "May you . . ." for "May I." For the last step substitute "May all beings or may all people everywhere . . ."

One of the beauties of this practice is that you can repeat these phrases in day-to-day life when you notice negative emotions arising toward yourself or another. For example, if someone cuts you off in traffic and you immediately want to shout at them, notice that habitual reaction arising and send the person lovingkindness phrases instead: "May you be well, may you be happy . . ." This will dissipate the angry feelings, which only hurt your own self.

You might use these phrases when someone has just said something hurtful to you. Rather than sink into despair or repetitive negative thinking, you can send generous, caring phrases to yourself and shift your state. As you calm down and relax your body, you may see the situation from a new perspective, be able to communicate better, or just move on. If you tend to go to overeating or other behaviors to numb unpleasant feelings, lovingkindness practice can help break this cycle by offering an alternative. You can use these phrases anytime you are feeling distressed or want a boost of positive wishes and feelings.

Compassion in the Moment

Compassion is a heartfelt quality of wishing to ease the suffering of others or yourself. Compassionate behavior toward others contributes to society and makes us feel good. In this self-compassion practice you send phrases of lovingkindness to yourself to ease or end your suffering. This is helpful in times of stress or discomfort.

Compassion practices are very similar to lovingkindness practice. The following is a potent "in the moment" exercise that can be cultivated by practicing lovingkindness meditation and self-kindness. You can place a hand on your heart or elsewhere on your body, a caring touch, when you are practicing these meditations, which helps stimulate the flow of the caregiving hormone oxytocin.

Self-Compassion Practice

Try this self-compassion "in the moment" practice to ease the suffering from a distressed mind or heart.

1. *Notice when you are suffering. Acknowledge to yourself*—This is uncomfortable/painful.

2. *Remember that you are not isolated in experiencing these feelings.* This is part of the human condition. We all suffer at times.

3. *Take a Mindful Check-In. Notice your thoughts, feelings, and what your body feels like as a result. Incline your mind toward kindness and compassion. Put a hand over your heart or give yourself a hug or a caring touch elsewhere on your body to generate positive emotions.*

4. *Repeat any of the phrases "May I be peaceful," "May I be at ease," "May I be safe," "May I be filled with lovingkindness," "Everything will be okay," or another that makes you feel safe, reassured, and comforted.*

5. *Ask yourself, What do I truly need? What would be most nourishing for me in this moment? See if you can give that to yourself.*

If food or some other unhelpful soother is calling to you (and you know you aren't really hungry), a moment of self-kindness may be all you need.

Self-compassion practice calms down the nervous system. Acknowledging and labeling suffering helps the brain's main center of emotional activation, the amygdala, to stop firing as much; the hand on the heart further calms and brings comfort and a feeling of safety. The sincere, kind wish to ease your own suffering and that of others is a beautiful and powerful thing. It is health promoting and stimulates the reward center of the brain. It's usually easier to wish that for others, but practicing lovingkindness and self-compassion meditation helps us learn to turn the kindness back onto ourselves as well.

After practicing, in a less activated state, we can see more clearly if there is a plan or course of action that is called for to ease our suffering. This includes seeking appropriate help if there is a true threat to physical or emotional safety in the home or other environments.

You can also send lovingkindness phrases to others, with the specific intent to ease their suffering using the format of the lovingkindness meditation. A hug, a comforting hand, a smile, kind words, and actions are all ways to express compassion and soothe another.

Scanning for Threats

When we are not relaxed and resting in spacious mind, the default of our normal everyday consciousness (in what researchers have termed the "negativity bias") is to scan for "threats" to our survival—what is not working, what needs to be fixed, a worry, a fear. This can leave us feeling vaguely unsafe, not at ease, or threatened in some way. Whether something is actually happening in the outside world or it's simply the comings and goings of imagined thoughts of the past or future, the body doesn't know the difference. Challenging emotions and thoughts can spiral, signaling a perceived danger. This can lead to the stress response.

Generally we are safe in the moment; it's just our mind firing thoughts. Bringing in a sense of safety through mindfulness and self-compassion practice can be very powerful to counteract the stress arousal and "suffering" in the body and mind. With this we can see clearly and plan for actions that are actually called for.

Savor the Good

When we notice what is positive and working in our lives, we feel better than when we focus on the negative. Our mind and body give us messages that things are all right and we can relax more. We can retrain our brains to focus more on the positive by savoring these types of moments and experiences. When you become aware of a positive experience, quality, emotion, thought, or beauty, give yourself time to enjoy it as you might a delicious apricot, plum, or square of dark chocolate. Feel the goodness of that experience. In fact, you might notice a pleasant memory arising while eating a particular food. You can relish that, letting the warmth of the memory nourish you, along with the actual food you are eating.

Similarly, we can evoke feelings of gratitude, appreciation, and joy. Don't let the precious moments of your life slip away underappreciated or unnoticed! Even when you are in a daily routine, you can find moments that are special. Bringing an open, inquisitive mind to all of your experiences helps keep things fresh. If everything is looking drab on the outside, you can also bring forth health-promoting feelings by simply remembering, evoking what you are grateful for in your life. Let the sense of appreciation fill your heart. It may even lead you to feelings of joy and awe.

Call Forth Positive Emotions

1. *In your Well Nourished Journal write each of the following qualities at the top of a page:*

   ~ *What you appreciate in your life*

   ~ *Everything that brings you joy*

   ~ *Everything that you feel grateful for*

2. *Fill each page for three minutes, listing and/or describing each quality. Move on when you've completed each.*

3. *Review each page, whatever its length, and soak in the good feelings that result. Remember to notice these regularly in your life and seek them out when they're absent.*

Focus on Self-Care and the Beauty in Life

The more you practice compassion toward yourself and elicit positive emotions regularly, the more you want to take better care of yourself. Make yourself more of a priority and you might find it effortless to do what it takes to practice healthy lifestyle habits. You may also notice you want to care more for others and the planet. Self-compassion is ultimately more of a motivator to take positive action in your life than sending negative thoughts and criticism toward yourself. Lovingkindess and compassion practices bring us out of an active judgmental mind state into a caring, resourced, and nourished place.

Beauty is tremendously nourishing, particularly if we take the time to notice and marinate in it! It can be all around you, even in a drop of water reflecting the sunlight, or a newly opening flower. Acknowledging the beauty in everyday things has been found to make a difference in mood and even in longevity when studied in the elderly. Nature has always been a source of beauty, inspiration, calm, and balance for humankind, especially when we feel safe and at ease. Savoring nature for its beauty and gifts, even if it's just that drop of water you noticed sparkling in the sunlight, can make a difference in your mood.

Receive the Gift

Joanna Macy, a noted Buddhist scholar and champion for the earth, offers the simple phrase "receive the gift" when out in nature. When you are outside, practice a mindful walk of whatever length. Pause occasionally and let your eyes be called to some object in nature. Take this in, saying silently to yourself, "Receive the gift." Nature not only has its own beauty that we can drink in; it also offers us messages through the metaphors of its own shapes if we just pay attention. Once while on a mindful walk, I paused and beheld a tree with bark of its own unique filigree. Superimposed upon a more usual linear bark pattern were swirls upon swirls. The tree as it grew created these complex patterns. It made me think of the imperfections of our bodies as we go through life, and how these can be celebrated and seen as beautiful and diverse like the variety of bark etchings and "imperfections" on trees.

Mindfulness of Challenging Emotions

When you notice you are distressed, a tendency may be to override the feelings and continue with your usual activities, to resist the uncomfortable feelings. You might drown them in ice cream, chocolate, or a shopping spree. You might find you are irritable and react with a sharp voice, defensiveness, or anger at the slightest hurt or perceived infraction.

You can meet the moment with a subtle but powerful reorientation to "welcome" an unpleasant feeling rather than push it away. An open, allowing attention helps counteract the energy of struggle and resistance that arises when we try to avoid a feeling or judge it. This gentle attention to feelings can have its own surprises. When we take the layer of resistance off, our suffering can decrease. Even if the feeling is still there, it will often decrease in intensity, shift in some way or transform, and pass through as all feelings eventually do. When we embrace an unpleasant feeling with kindness, our judging and reactive mind tends to become quieter as well. The space that is created enables us to see clearly if there is anything that needs attending to. Rather than eat or engage in some other unhelpful activity, we can find a moment of peace and perspective to simply be and allow any wise choices to emerge.

Surf the Urge with Lovingkindness

A powerful, mindful way to stay present and calm in the midst of the rising, ebbing, and falling waves of your emotions and cravings has been called "surfing the urge" by Alan Marlatt. The analogy of a wave is helpful. You meet the presence of your feelings with a calm, clear attention. With curiosity you explore the shape, the sensations, the size of the feeling and where you sense it in the body. This begins a process of dis-identification, where you are no longer in the middle of the feeling. You see it from a little distance, gaining a healthy perspective that the feeling is not you but a passing companion or visitor. As you stay present with the feeling and explore it in this way, the intensity and size tend to go down—what we might imagine surfing a wave to be like. This process can be particularly self-evident with urges and cravings. They don't last forever; they crest and fall away.

When we add lovingkindness practice, the shift in craving is particularly potent. The resulting space and perspective allow for greater insight and freedom from the craving. This practice is a favorite among my clients and workshop participants.

The following practice uses the skills of mindfulness, surfing the urge, and lovingkindness to work with strong food cravings that result particularly from stress or strong emotions. This practice is most effective after you have had some experience and proficiency with mindfulness and lovingkindness practice.

Feed Cravings with Kindness Practice

1. Close your eyes and imagine a food you tend to crave (or look at it, if it's in front of you), particularly when a strong emotion such as anxiety or a challenging situation is a trigger. As the image of the food becomes more vivid, notice the craving growing stronger.

2. Notice where the feeling of craving is in the body and explore the shape, size, and sensation of the craving or urge with curiosity and kindness.

3. Imagine a sense of lovingkindness growing in your heart (as in the practice introduced earlier) and filling your body.

4. Envelop the craving in warmth and lovingkindness. Staying with that, put a hand on your heart if you wish (and/or repeat some lovingkindness phrases to yourself).

5. Rest in that sense of warmth and lovingkindness. After a while, look at or imagine the food again and notice if anything has changed.

This practice helps you get control back, and the craving goes down significantly or disappears completely. People are surprised how quickly this happens and that it can happen at all! Perhaps the most profound aspect of this practice is that people often realize, from the inside out, that what they are really craving is love and that they are trying to get it unsuccessfully from the food. When they offer themselves the love, kindness, and self-compassion inherent in this exercise, they become filled with the wellsprings of their own heart.

ALLOWS for Mindfulness of Emotions

This process builds upon and sums up many of the practices introduced above.

A—Acknowledge you have difficult emotions present. Recognize them without judgment.

L—Label and identify your emotion(s). Research has shown that simply by identifying an emotion, reactivity in the amygdala goes down.

L—ALlow the feelings, sensations, and thoughts associated with the emotion to just be. Stop the fight, the resistance, the struggle, letting them melt away.

O—Expl**O**re or inquire into your experience. Any sensations or shape to the emotion? Where is it located in your body? Is there a belief or thought connected to the emotion? The emotion may already have changed and shifted in some way from the first few steps. Watch how the thoughts may pass on through, releasing their hold on the emotion.

W—Wide view or vie**W**point, a new perspective and space, will emerge. You see and experience with inner eyes that you are not that feeling or thought. In that fresh space is freedom and new possibilities for choice.

S—Self-care. Is there anything else you need right now? Just this breath, this moment of peace coming into the present, where everything is "okay"? A positive action step? Offer yourself some lovingkindness phrases, or perhaps some self-care, nourishing activities, or communication with another.

Nourishing Activities List

With the self-kindness, space, and perspective that are cultivated by the different practices we have visited, it can be helpful to have a ready list of nourishing activities you can engage in to further shift your emotional body toward full nourishment and what it truly needs. In the more resourced space you have created within yourself, ask yourself, What do I really need? Listen to your inner wisdom. Resting in your natural resourced awareness may be enough. But with perspective and clarity you may see you are hungry for something else. Use the List of Nourishing Activities you created in chapter 4 to help you, and add to the list as you like. Focus on activities that particularly enhance your mood (e.g., being in nature, connecting with a friend, a cozy blanket, and a good book); doing something good for yourself or for others, getting out of the house or office, and shifting perspective can make a difference.

Mindful Eating

Eating a food, snack, or meal with full presence can be emotionally nourishing. Check into how hungry you are and make your choices accordingly. Take time to make your inner and outer environment appealing. Nourish yourself with a few breaths, filling with gratitude and appreciation for what you're about to eat. Eat and savor with all your senses. When you open to receive the emotional and psychological nourishment of a meal, you may find that you won't need to eat as much as you usually do. The whole experience becomes nurturing and even joyful.

Sometimes pleasant memories arise when eating a certain food. We can let these nourish our experience as well. If unpleasant memories consistently arise with a certain food, the wise choice may be to not eat that food, or you might work skillfully with the thoughts as introduced in the next chapter.

Your SPRIGS Goals

Create several SPRIGS goals to support the inner nourishment of your emotional body. Revisit and assess periodically how you are doing and adjust accordingly.

_____

_____

_____

_____

OUTER SUPPORT

How can you reach out and find support for your emotional body? You can nurture your social connections, savor a shared smile or impromptu conversation with a coworker or friend. Share with your check-in buddy. Nourish with beauty; you can take in the sights, the sounds, the details of daily life as if you've never noticed them before—observe the world around you and notice its beauty. Are there special touches you can add to your house, your workspace, even your car to make it more nurturing and beautiful? Perhaps you might organize and discard clutter that you no longer need. Add plants, pictures, objects of nature, throw rugs—a few lovely items that elicit a happy or joyful feeling in you could make your environment more harmonious. Maybe simply opening the curtains to a view of the trees or caring for an indoor plant could lift your mood.

Rest in the "enoughness," the "fullness," of a life well nourished from the inside out, as well as the outside in. Consider spending more time in nature, or at least pausing to savor nature when you see it and attune your emotional body to its nourishing effects. Not only the eyes behold beauty, but all the senses do in their own particular way. Open your senses to the wind, sound of the birds, buzzing of honeybees (hopefully), and the rustle of leaves in the trees. Treat yourself to the music of a bubbling stream, which is intrinsically soothing and heart-opening.

Use the planning tool SPRIGS to easefully introduce new practices and habits into your life.

INNER RESOURCES

The tools of emotional nourishment help keep us energized and positive in our day-to-day life. This support in turn helps us to reach our goals of mindful eating and living. The qualities of gratitude, lovingkindness, self-compassion, joy, and peace can be intentionally watered with our kind attention through these practices. With time, practice, and gentle, consistent effort they will bud, open, and flower in a fragrant, multihued bouquet of positive qualities. With greater ease we can call upon them to sweeten and enrich our days.

Some people find it helpful to have a regular bedtime or waking ritual to remember what they are grateful for. You can choose one of these positive qualities and make your own personal practice. When you go to bed at night or wake up in the morning, call to mind three things you feel grateful for or that bring you joy. They could be things that happened during the day or things you are looking forward to.

Use Your 5 Steps Prompter Tools

[ ] Fill in the emotional body in your Well Nourished Bowl.

[ ] Fill out your Intention and Goals Prompter for the emotional body.

[ ] Use your 5 Steps Daily Prompter to help support you in mindful choices.

CHAPTER SIX

Psychological Nourishment: Navigating Thoughts and Feelings

The flavor of our thoughts affects the quality of our moment-to-moment experience.

Psychological health includes mindfulness of our habitual thoughts, emotions, feelings, awareness, and reactivity. It includes the quality of our thoughts and feelings. Even more important, it involves our relationship to what is arising in our experiences. The flavor of our thoughts affects the quality of our moment-to-moment and day-to-day experience. When we are under stress, when the moments of our life don't meet our expectations, it is perfectly normal for more difficult thoughts and feelings to arise, which can lead to behaviors that aren't supportive of our well-being. That's one important reason to pay attention to thoughts and feelings—bringing mindful awareness to them can help us move away from their controlling us. We have more freedom to choose how we want to spice our day with skillful means and tools.

It's easy to get caught in a cycle of negative thoughts and feelings leading to stress and to engage in habitual behaviors to feel better, such as overeating, prolonged sedentary couch visits, endless striving, constant busyness, and procrastinating on completing meaningful projects or activities. You may also be in a seemingly endless cycle of striving and busyness fueled by societal, cultural, and personal beliefs. Busyness keeps you from connecting to yourself and others. All these behaviors are not actually giving you the true nourishment you need. You might find you judge yourself or have regret, anger, or disappointment. Further difficult thoughts and feelings can arise, leading to more unnourishing behaviors.

Without mindfulness, we can be at the mercy of the difficult thoughts and overlapping cycles that can emerge. The tools and practices in this chapter can help us return to and rest in our true, balanced nature. They help us navigate the sometimes rocky terrain of thoughts and feelings more skillfully, significantly decreasing the symptoms and impact of stress on our bodies and the resulting behaviors and habits we may have used to cope until now. (Note: If you have been experiencing negative thoughts that feel incapacitating or are significantly affecting usual function for more than two weeks, it is a good idea to seek medical advice or assessment from your doctor or a psychotherapist.)

What We Know

Many fields of scientific research are converging to show the different ways our thoughts, beliefs, and feelings can affect our biology—including our immune system, our genetic expressions, our digestion, absorption of nutrients, even the level of inflammation in our bodies. They also affect our mind and heart, not just our physical functions. But this is not a one-way relationship. How we nourish all of our "bodies," the different parts of ourselves and aspects of our lives, can affect our thoughts and feelings positively or negatively.

We understand how important it is to resource the physical body, feeding it with the proper balance of healthy food, sleep, relaxation, and exercise, and how that affects our outlook, well-being, thoughts, feelings, and behaviors. We have seen how working skillfully with emotions, nourishing and resourcing ourselves with practices to cultivate mindfulness, lovingkindness, compassion, and gratitude, can help us find emotional balance, joy, and ease.

With practice, you'll find over time that you no longer need to use food or other means as the predominant way to feel fulfilled. You'll know from the inside how these old ways of coping are not meeting what you are truly hungry for. They leave you with more of what you don't want—difficult thoughts, feelings, stress, and even extra weight. These habits have built up over years. It takes time to unwind them, and no one is perfect. When you do slip back occasionally, you can practice self-compassion.

First take a few moments to reflect, assess, and set an intention in this area.

AWARENESS

○ Pause ○ Reflect ○ Assess

Ask yourself the following questions.

~ *Do I feel confident that I have the skills and tools I need to navigate my psychological health?*

~ *Do I approach my experiences with kindness and compassion?*

~ *At any given time, do I tend to have more negative, neutral, or positive thoughts?*

~ *Do I tend to judge myself, my behaviors, thoughts, and feelings frequently?*

~ *Do I consider all of my thoughts to be absolutely true?*

~ *Do I frequently feel stuck in my thoughts and feelings?*

~ *Does this get in the way of living my life in a positive, meaningful way?*

~ *Does this impact the kinds of choices I make to take care of myself?*

If you answered no to either of the first two questions or yes to any of the last six questions, you have room to nourish your psychological body.

Mindful Check-In

What do I notice is affecting the health of my psychological body in this moment? What thoughts, feelings, and bodily sensations am I aware of now? How have I eaten today? Did I sleep enough? When did I last exercise? What was the last quality social connection that I had? What is happening in this moment, in my day, in my life? What skills do I have to help me come back to balance?

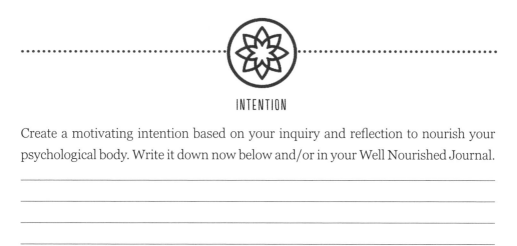

INTENTION

Create a motivating intention based on your inquiry and reflection to nourish your psychological body. Write it down now below and/or in your Well Nourished Journal.

_____

_____

_____

_____

We'll now explore the terrain of your thoughts more intimately and how proven mindfulness and cognitive behavioral approaches can help nourish your mind, improving psychological health (and thus emotional and physical health). You'll learn how to put your awareness in the driver's seat so you can direct your life and not be at the whim of passing thoughts, emotions, and feelings.

The Truth of How Our Mind Works

Psychologists and researchers today accept that we have a negativity bias. In order to survive over the thousands of years of our evolution, being able to respond to immediate dangers and challenges was an advantage. Our minds have evolved to be constantly scanning for threats to our survival. Neuroscience studies show that our brains react more strongly to negative stimuli than positive stimuli. This means you'll notice and remember the negative things that happen to you more than the positive if your mind is left to its own devices. In fact, you'll tend to revisit and focus on what is not working, or anything you feel worried or unsettled about. This is evolution's way of making sure you attend to being safe first and foremost. This, coupled with the mind's natural tendency to wander when not focused on tasks or activities, can bring you back again and again to what isn't working. You'll then focus on the lowest-hanging fruit of discord, a tendency that escalates when you feel out of balance or stressed.

What are some of your lowest-hanging fruits? Are you overly focused on your weight, food, or body image? When you feel stressed, even just a low level of anxiety, is that where your mind habitually goes? "If only I lost ten pounds my life would be so much better . . ." Or you might be revisiting every angle and future possibility of the current problem of the day. Focusing on these thoughts and engaging with them creates unhappiness and dissatisfaction in the present moment. A string of these moments makes up your experience of life. How much more useful it would be to notice this tendency as part of the negativity bias. Are these thoughts helpful, nourishing, motivating, joyful?

With knowledge and awareness we can recognize that this is the normal default pattern in our minds. There is nothing wrong with us—we all experience this to varying degrees and intensities. What becomes a problem is when we are wedded to all our thoughts and stories as absolutely true; when we don't know how to get out of the ruminative cycles that arise; when we don't question our self-limiting beliefs and judgments. Living a well-nourished life with mindfulness at its foundation gives us the resources to offset this pattern.

If you take a closer look, you may notice that in fact you have similar thoughts, beliefs, and stories arising in response to events around you as you did years ago. Are these empowering, energizing responses to the daily challenges around you? Or are they giving you similar results in your life from repeating familiar behaviors? Would you like to learn ways of nourishing yourself with new stories, new possibilities, and at the very least to be free of the ways of thinking that no longer serve you? Mindfulness and other approaches can help.

Stress and the Mind-Body Connection

Besides thoughts affecting your moods, level of happiness, fulfillment, and satisfaction, they can actually affect your biology. A groundbreaking study revealed that the stress responses of caregivers in similar situations affected their biology, depending on the level of their negative outlook and self-reported stress levels. The caregivers' telomeres, which are the caps at the end of the chromosomes and which get shorter as we grow older, much like a cap on a shoelace, were shorter in those who reported more extreme feelings of stress. This was the first study showing that our subjective experience of stress actually can affect the rate at which we age.

A key way to manage stress is to shift your perspective to one that is more positive and life affirming. This leads to positive emotions that open the door wide to possibilities rather than slamming the door shut with thoughts that include "always," "never," or "only." This type of thinking almost always is self-limiting with generalizations such as "I can never be healthier" or "I always sabotage myself." This chapter will teach ways to challenge these types of thoughts.

Negative thinking and emotions related to survival and stress threats narrow our focus and field of possibility in our minds and actions. We expend huge amounts of mental and life energy by being caught in these cycles. That energy can be freed up when you have skillful means to focus on what you love and appreciate in your life, including the difference you want to make in your world (from the personal to the planetary). Feeding your whole self with what you truly need supports a more positive outlook as well. When you feel good, healthy, and nourished, your outlook will always be brighter.

SKILLS AND TOOLS

The greatest freedom and nourishment is the ability to rest in ourselves peacefully and be present fully in the moment. In spacious awareness, we feel full and complete. But we inhabit human bodies and do have physical needs, so this is a wonderful place from which to make our self-care choices.

Regular practice in spacious awareness helps strengthen your ability to see clearly what is arising in the mind, what is helpful and what is not. Sometimes what is unfolding, what is rippling through the mind, feels so solid at first, and then sometimes so fleeting. When you anchor your attention in spacious awareness, you will attain a more true, felt sense of yourself. You can more easily choose where to put your attention and where to let go.

Hopefully you have set aside some time each day to practice mindfulness meditation and rest in spacious mind (or spacious awareness), as introduced in the previous chapter. If you haven't, consider finding a time and place each day to practice following the guidelines for setting up a regular practice in chapter 4.

We typically think of wisdom as arising from the mind. But it's not the only source of wisdom in the body. Three sources of wisdom do contribute to psychological health, especially when we pay attention and listen. These are sometimes called the three brains.

Wisdom of the Mind

Wisdom of the mind doesn't necessarily come from the thoughts themselves. It arises from a deeper place. We have a vast reservoir of untapped wisdom that becomes more accessible to us when we take time out in our busy lives. A shift of perspective, an insight, a new idea can arise and bubble up not only while we are meditating but in the in-between moments of our focused, task-oriented attention. Take a moment to pause in your day, to mindfully sip a glass of bubbly water with a slice of lime, to relish in the moments of beauty and joy, to walk outside. We don't need to force positive thoughts and insights; they come as a gift when the mind is not caught up in chatter, stress, or worry. This deeper knowing can guide our daily decisions, and our overall thoughts will also be clearer.

Wisdom of the Heart

Your heart knows. The heart is a seat of intelligence in its own right. It has the same receptors for neurotransmitters and peptides, the same molecules of emotion that the brain and the gut have. Take the time to listen to your heart's knowing and factor this into your decisions and actions. Sometimes practical reality, logistics, or finances make it difficult to follow your heart, at least immediately. If you are unsure of a decision, rest your awareness in the area of your heart. Does it rise, feel open and uplifted, or sink or constrict when you think of a pending choice or action? You can use this as a guide to balance decisions with your thinking mind, particularly when the thoughts are arising from a mindful, calm place.

The heart is often associated with intuition. It may have more information than the thinking mind about the future outcome of your choices. It has your best interest at heart.

Think back in your own life to when your heart has served you as a guide. Most of us have had the experience that if we had listened to our heart, we would have made a wiser choice. And we can look back and see how listening to our heart led to positive outcomes. What would it be like to live a life following your heart's path? Sometimes we need to work on challenging our limiting beliefs, both conscious and subconscious, to be able to do so!

Wisdom of the Gut

The digestive tract has its own nervous system called the enteric nervous system, which has many receptors for the same neurotransmitters found in the brain. The gut is sometimes called our second brain. As mentioned in chapter 2, the connection between the brain and the gut goes two ways. The health of your gut and digestion can affect your moods, just as stress and other emotions can affect your digestion. You may experience feelings in your gut before your thinking mind has even processed a situation. This connection has been recognized in our language by expressions such as "I have a gut feeling" or "Go with your gut."

Listen to the wisdom of your gut. It responds to your perception of stress through the information it receives from your thoughts, emotions, and subconscious. It also gives you information on nourishing your psychological body, if you listen. What we eat can affect our moods and the health of our microbiome. When you pay attention to your digestive system, it gives you cues about what does or doesn't sit well with you. Bring awareness to your entire body during and after eating and note what nourishes your mind. Practice mindful eating. Consider trying new nutrient-rich foods that support psychological wellness and balance (see page 32).

Mindfulness of Thoughts

What about the contents of your thoughts and how your perception of events influences your level of stress and reactivity? The following practices home in on ways to skillfully work with thoughts and their content.

This mindfulness practice helps you become less identified with your thoughts as always being true. It helps you see how your thoughts are not you. When you watch your mind, you are able to experience its transient nature firsthand. This practice helps inform the Mindful Check-In and mindful pause practice in your daily life.

Mindfulness of Thoughts

1. Begin your sitting meditation practice by focusing your attention on the breath. Notice what area of the breath feels most easy to rest your attention upon. Be curious about the texture, sensation, and duration of the breath.

2. Each time you notice your attention has wandered, meet each new object of attention with kindness and without judgment. Then return your attention to the breath.

3. Shift your attention to simply watching thoughts as they arise without further engaging in the content. Let go of any judging. See if you can notice the beginning, the middle, and the end of the thoughts. Notice them as mental events with a discrete beginning and ending. If this feels too difficult at first, simply notice them as passing like clouds. Thoughts just come and go. The content is not necessarily true.

Labeling

You can try labeling your thoughts in the following practice, which helps develop steady attention and decrease the tendency to react to whatever is arising in the mind. This is useful when we practice meeting the moment in our lives with a mindful pause or the ALLOWS process. Your mindfulness grows stronger than the inevitable eating or other triggers you may encounter around or within you. You have more choice if they pull you away from your intentions and how you want to respond.

Basic Labeling

1. Gently anchor the attention on the breath and note silently "in breath" and "out breath" with each breath.

2. Expand to label whatever you notice arising in the mind—thoughts, feelings, emotions, sound. You might note "thinking," "feeling," "sound," or be more specific: "planning," "memory," "sad," "happy."

Try this practice occasionally or regularly in your sitting meditation. Many people prefer to just notice what's arising with kind attention and return to the breath without "labeling."

Past or Future

Labeling your thoughts as either "past" or "future" when they arise can be a simple yet particularly powerful way of returning to awareness of the present moment. You may notice a slight resistance that arises when you first try this practice. It's almost as if we have a set level of comfort for resting in the present moment. Our minds tend to fly off to fretting about something or planning for the future, taking us away from the present moment unnecessarily. This practice is a good training ground to increase our capacity to stay in the present moment with more ease.

1. Begin with the basic labeling practice.
2. Label whatever you notice arising in the mind. Now use the label "past" or "future" for these thoughts, images, memories. You might notice how much you attach to your thoughts. What is the level of struggle or drama in the present moment? How difficult does it feel to let go of wrestling with your mind?
3. Continue labeling "past" or "future" and returning to the present moment. You may be surprised at how easy it is to keep coming back to the powerful present with this practice. Just allow for the initial difficulty of moving out of your current comfort zone and into a greater level of peace.

With practice you will slowly be able to create a new set point, a place of more peace and tranquility that you can return to when the waves of life hit, either in your mind or in outside events and circumstances.

Let's look at a possible real-life situation. You are in a mall, and the smell of those cinnamon buns is overpowering. You remember how your grandmother used to bake these on the weekends. You want one now. But you stop and take a mindful pause. You check in to what is true for you in this moment. You are grounded firmly in your mindfulness and awareness. You take in the pleasant feelings of those memories and notice it makes you feel happy. You recognize that you are not hungry and in fact are feeling quite full from lunch. You are aware of the thoughts, feelings, and sensations from the past, and note "past" to yourself. You breathe in the aroma of those buns and feel almost ecstatic with the deliciousness. You feel whole and complete and walk on by. I have enjoyed moments like this over the years in our malls. Several times I've made a different choice and enjoyed half a bun or so mindfully without any guilt.

Challenging Your Thoughts, Creating Positive Intentions

We can intentionally choose more positive thoughts and ways of thinking to nourish our minds. Mindful awareness helps us see the patterns and types of thoughts. The following tools help us challenge the content and bring in new ways of seeing.

Challenge the Thought

Sometimes emotions or stress are our first clue that our thoughts are not nourishing. As we learned from the stress and telomere study, our perceptions of a situation and the resources we bring to cope make a huge difference in our biology. Notice what your perception is of a stressful situation. Is it truly accurate? If not, what is more accurate?

1. Notice a difficult thought or belief clouding your mind, or perhaps a rainstorm of thoughts hailing down. Pause, breathe.
2. Write down the predominant thought(s) arising. Ask yourself, How true is this thought? Am I exaggerating this situation, reality, in any way? Am I caught in a loop of blaming myself or another? Am I overgeneralizing this one difficult situation or belief, applying it to the rest of my life?
3. Take another breath. Spend a moment just being aware of your breath. Ask yourself, Do I need to look for evidence to the contrary of this belief or thought to help me let go? Think about the circumstances surrounding this negative, unhelpful thought. Use the evidence gathered to help you in the next step.
4. Think about the bigger picture of your life. Is there a more positive and energizing way to think about this situation, yourself, another? What is the kind, compassionate thought? Write that down. Make it as believable as you can, using any real-life evidence you have gathered.
5. If a version of the first thought floats back in, meet it gently with kindness, so it won't take hold of your attention. Ask yourself, How would I feel in this moment without this thought? What would my life be like without this thought? Can I let go of it?

6. Bring yourself back to the present moment with awareness of your breath, of your body's sensations and position—whether sitting, standing, walking. Just notice you are here right now—okay and safe. No need to "future" or "past" in this moment. Remind yourself of the energizing thought. If there is a new action that follows, celebrate that!

Even in a situation that seems all negative, there is usually some possibility of good or eventual positive outcome we can notice. Changing our beliefs, our perceptions, invites positive emotions. Those that view the world more as a good place than a bad place are happier. We can see why training our minds to incline toward the good and savor it is so nourishing.

Take a Thought Breather

Every now and then you may catch yourself in a loop of thoughts, accompanied by a torrent of unpleasant emotions and feelings. At that moment, depending upon the intensity and what activities you are engaged in, you can simply say to yourself, "STOP. Let go," "No thank you." or "This isn't helpful." You might visualize the word stop if you like. In that pause and interruption of the stream, take a few breaths. Come back to the present moment. Then assess what wise action is called for in this moment. Perhaps you will practice ALLOWS, lovingkindness meditation, or a self-compassion practice. Perhaps it's engaging in another activity or positive distraction. A change of scenery. Maybe it's a moment to attend to some business or errands you have been putting off, or make a specific plan for them later.

Proclaim Your Well-Being

Regular positive affirmations to sow greater health, wholesome qualities, and states of mind can give your conscious and subconscious mind a map to follow in your daily life. You can choose to follow a maze of possibilities in any moment of your life. Our brain thrives on novelty. When you are in a daily routine or ritual of work that is not that interesting or satisfying, your mind might look for stimulation through food, drink, caffeine, or TV. But you can feed novelty in a different kind of way. With a diet of positive, nourishing thoughts, you'll be inclined toward taking the more uplifting step in your life. You'll see new possibilities.

Repeating positive phrases is most effective when we are in a relaxed frame of mind. The two sides of our brain can speak to each other better. Our subconscious gets the message as well as our conscious mind. Instead of our minds subtly or not-so-subtly scanning for what is not working in default mode (the negativity bias), we program our minds to seek out steps, information, actions, and people that support our positive declarations. Out of the cultivation of wholesome qualities and nurturing intentions, our visions and dreams manifest step-by-step. When we really pay attention, we see it's all here right now in this moment.

○ Affirm ○ Proclaim ○ Declare

1. Use lovingkindness phrases liberally in your day-to-day life—say them when you wake up in the morning, when you go to bed. Use them in moments of self-compassion and for self-care after the ALLOWS process.
2. Try rephrasing or making them feel more like your own: "I am healthy and happy in this moment." "I accept myself just as I am right now."
3. During periods of intentional mindful activities during your day—walking, sitting, gardening, standing—pair positive phrases with the in breath and the out breath. For example, [breathing in] "I am calm," [breathing out] "I feel peace," [breathing in] "I forgive myself," [breathing out] "I let go, and love myself again," [breathing in] "Everything will be okay," [breathing out] "All is well in this moment."

Positive phrases nourish the mind. When you practice, you will notice the calm, peace, even joy that result. It's contagious. Your calm and joyful presence will soothe and inspire others.

Shake Off the Resistance

When it feels particularly hard to affirm a positive statement or to try a new, positive step in your life, you probably have counterbeliefs or lack the skills and knowledge to create the support structure to achieve it. Write about it or talk to a friend or trusted counselor. In a safe, comfortable place, shake out physically any counterbeliefs you become aware of, dance them out, shout them out. Then affirm the new beliefs or positive statements loudly. Common counterbeliefs run at a level just below our usual awareness at first but are more obvious once we become aware of their existence. These include beliefs such as "I'm not good enough," "I am bad," or "I am unlovable," which are not the truth of who we really are. We all have some variation of these internalized from childhood. They get activated at moments of shame, insecurity, stress, or uncertainty. For some the intensity may be stronger, for some the number of beliefs greater. These core negative beliefs can get watered by our negativity bias! You can create beliefs to directly counter these and meet resistance with these tips.

ALLOWS

You can now revisit the ALLOWS process, which was introduced in chapter 5 (page 104), adding new skills to work directly with the unhelpful or negative thoughts that arise. The ALLOWS process also helps us to become aware of our sneaky core negative beliefs and of the thoughts fueling them.

Close your eyes and take a few centering breaths. Imagine a recent situation that brings up some challenging feelings for you.

A—Acknowledge the difficult emotions present.

L—Label and identify the emotions.

L—ALlow the feelings, sensations, and thoughts just to be.

O—ExplO**re** or inquire into your experience. Is there a belief or thought connected to the emotion? *If the thought or belief is still strong, even stubborn, try challenging that belief using the "challenge the thought" practice above. "How true is this thought?" Write down this step, then put the new compassionate and kind thought in the Self-Care step when you arrive there.*

W—Wide view and a new perspective emerge.

S—Self-Care. Ask yourself, Is there anything else I need right now? Savor the new space that has likely been created. *You may like to offer yourself a "new belief," some lovingkindness phrases, affirmations, and/or reassertion of an intention. Create a new belief phrase designed to counter a core negative belief you became aware of: "Everything is okay," "I am lovable," "I am safe," "It's okay just to rest and be in this moment," "There is nothing I have to do or be right now."*

Notice which of the practices we've learned call to you and consider adding some specific practices for your goals and intentions using the SPRIGS process. As you become comfortable with some, begin to add more.

Your SPRIGS Goals

Add any new goals or adjust the ones you have for this area using SPRIGS and the ways to nourish your psychological body. Each week it's helpful to revisit and assess how you are doing and adjust accordingly.

_____

_____

_____

_____

OUTER SUPPORT

Write down your lovingkindness phrases and positive affirmations and put them up as reminders around your workspace, in your calendar, or on Web reminder notes. Record positive and loving messages to yourself on your phone and play them back at needed times during the day. Put up a note that says "open" or "breathe" as a reminder to yourself to open and relax into the moment when you notice you are resisting it. Make the time to practice ALLOWS or other exercises in this chapter. Choose an object that is pleasant or comforting to you and put it on your desk or in your purse as a reminder to stop and take a thought breather when you need it. Practice lovingkindness to help you be more attuned and compassionate to others and yourself. Self-compassion practice can help you reach out when feeling down. Nurture and draw upon your social support—your connections and community— as the quality of your social connections greatly impacts your psychological body. Plan nourishing social activities. Attend a meditation group. Use the planning tool SPRIGS to easefully introduce new practices and habits into your life.

INNER RESOURCES

Nourish the ground of your being with positive qualities, nutritious thoughts, and affirmations through daily practice. Revisit and proclaim your intentions that you set in each chapter of the book to feed and care for all the parts of yourself. These positive statements worded powerfully for your own well-being can be used as affirmations as well. Review your Well Nourished Journal or what you write in this book regularly. Keep your intentions in mind. Call them forth to direct your choices and carry you through the maze of possibilities. They cue both your conscious and subconscious mind to notice everything that aligns with them. Support gets magnetized to you; synchronicities and coincidences can abound. Opportunities for nourishment are seemingly everywhere. Self-compassion practice will help keep you motivated to maintain or begin new beneficial activities and help draw support.

Use Your 5 Steps Prompter Tools

[ ] Fill in the psychological body in your Well Nourished Bowl.

[ ] Fill out your Intention and Goals Prompter for the psychological body.

[ ] Use your 5 Steps Daily Prompter to help support you in mindful choice.

CHAPTER SEVEN

Social Nourishment: Building Relationships and Community

Social connections nourish happiness and health—there are many ways to weave your basket full of this important ingredient.

Your social connections can be a tremendous source of nourishment. They are increasingly recognized in research as a very important element in health, well-being, and success. This includes feeling connected to a circle of family and friends, to work, and to community. Feeling connected to ourselves is equally important. When we are feeling resourced, calm, and balanced we are more available to nurture and support others, which in turn nurtures and deepens our capacity for more meaningful relationships.

Social connection is so important to our development that "failure to thrive" in infants and children who receive no caring human touch, love, or attention is recognized among health care professionals. It gives us a sense of belonging, of being needed, and the opportunity to make a difference in others' lives. Warm, kind, loving engagement with others stimulates our own internal apothecary of well-being in ways we are just beginning to understand.

For some, relationships come easily. Others struggle with relational, social, and emotional skills. Still others focus more on meaningful work and projects than relationships and yet seem to fare well, not suffering any consequences of fewer or less frequent social connections. Understanding the benefits of positive connection with yourself and others can motivate you to take steps—such as the practices in this book—to improve your relationships wherever you are in this spectrum. You can develop the capacity to be a great friend to yourself as well as to others, who may not always be available in a moment of need.

What We Know

The quality and quantity of our ongoing social connections and involvements directly impact our physical, mental, emotional, and spiritual health. If this is an area in which you are undernourished, you can learn to improve your relational and communication skills, and to apply strategies that strengthen your social connections.

The good news is that it's not just about quantity of relationships, both in person and online. Some people are naturally introverts. It's the subjective experience of our social connections that's the most important. If you tend to be more solitary but are deeply resourced from inside, with only a few close relationships, you may feel satisfied and nourished enough in this area of your life.

If you are frustrated with your ability to deepen and sustain friendships, or to make new friends, the skills outlined in this chapter can help. In surprising recent research, 25 percent of adults reported they do not have anyone to confide in. That is one in four adults! In this same study, the average number of confidants that adults had was one.

People with less perceived social support can have higher rates of anxiety, depression, and other potential health problems over time. The quality of your relationships trumps quantity in other important ways too. Social connections that are stressful can increase inflammation in the body. Discernment in your relationships; having tools, outer support, and inner resources; and feeling empowered to set healthy boundaries can help.

We know that good-quality social connections improve mood, happiness, overall health, and length of life. We can even recover from illness quicker. Social connectivity can contribute to a sense of personal worthiness and belonging.

In practical terms we enjoy more hugs, fulfilling conversation, sharing fun events or exercising together, having someone to call in times of need, and sharing both everyday and momentous events. Having more social support can also lead to greater resource sharing and self-care information that may also impact health. It can help you be more successful as you change your behavior to improve your overall well-being. In fact, it has such a helpful effect that it is included in one of the 5 steps in this book: Outer Support.

There is no one formula for what your social network should look like. We are unique individuals with different relationship styles and needs, temperaments, and personalities. You may be naturally more introverted or shy; you may be more extroverted and outgoing. You may thrive on having lots of social connections, or you may have just a few close friends around you. Some people are naturally more independent; others define sense of self-worth through relationships and needing to be needed. You may be in a long-term, committed partnership with a significant other, wanting to find that special partner (dating or not), or perhaps in a place where that is not important to you. Your perception of the quality of your social support will vary depending upon who you are and your skills and needs. What are the specific areas you want to enrich? Would you like to focus on having more rewarding relationships? Would you like to cultivate a larger network of support and mutually meaningful connections? Are you satisfied currently?

AWARENESS

○ Pause ○ Reflect ○ Assess

Take a moment now to reflect on the following questions to see which areas of nourishment are lacking or fulfilling in your social body.

~ How nourishing are my social connections?

~ Do I have one or more people I can confide in on a regular basis?

~ Do I have people in my life I can enjoy activities with regularly?

~ Do I have a sense of involvement in a community greater than myself?

~ Are my connections rewarding and positive?

~ Do I have laughter in my life?

~ Am I contributing in a meaningful way to others?

~ Can I count on myself to be there for me?

If you answered no to any of these questions, then you will benefit by enriching your social body with the skills, tools, and practices in this book.

Mindful Check-In

What is the quality of my experience when I am feeling connected to others? To my-self? When I am feeling alone? What do I notice in my thoughts, feelings, and physical sensations? Do I notice I eat when I am feeling lonely or isolated instead of from true physical hunger? How does feeling socially connected affect my physical experience?

INTENTION

Create an intention(s) based on your reflections above to increase nourishment of your social connections. This can include connection with yourself. Write these down now here and/or in your Well Nourished Journal.

_____

_____

_____

As you read through this next section, choose the areas to focus on that feel most pertinent to you.

Mindful Connecting, Nourishing Communication

Let's take a look at the different components that can improve and deepen the positive, warm engagements in your life.

Empathy and Compassion. Empathy is a natural human attribute. Our brain is wired to respond to another's pain and joy, and to feel someone else's experience as our own to varying degrees. We feel connected through empathy, but the more busy or stressed we are, the more we tend to focus on ourselves to just get by. The stress response heightens our drive for self-preservation, and our focus tends to narrow. When this happens, you may not be very available for others, to pause, listen, and receive. Coming back to your breath, to awareness of your body, your senses, to a mindful pause, helps you be open to the other person. When we experience empathy, neurons in our brain, called mirror neurons, light up that reflect the actions of the other person. They are part of a complex brain process that allows us to imagine and feel, to resonate with, another person's emotional experience as our own. We could even say that when we feel empathy for another, aspects of our brains mirror each other.

Compassion is the wish for another person's suffering to end. It is an indomitable force and expression of our shared humanity. You may experience it as your heart going out to someone, or wanting to make it better for another. You might offer suggestions or take action to help ease your friend's, beloved's, or a stranger's suffering. Practicing self-compassion also helps increase your compassion for others. We feel more connected when we hold compassion for one another.

Kindness and Self-Kindness. Practicing kindness to yourself does not always come easily. It's often easier to practice kindness with others before yourself. Yet when you are feeling good and resourced, you can be kind and present for others.

We live in a social milieu with all kinds of cultural messages of what is acceptable or not acceptable, about our looks, clothes, body size, tastes. We may have gotten messages from the media, a parent, or others that our body type or size is not okay. You may notice when you pay attention, a significant proportion of your thoughts are judgmental or compare you to others or a cultural standard. This can get in the way of being kind to others as well as yourself.

Kindness to yourself includes not paying attention to the habitual negative thoughts that may arise about your body, your shape, or your weight and not comparing yourself to others. Let go of the judgmental thoughts and come back to the moment by recognizing and awakening out of the thought train you may have been on. Choose where you want to put your thoughts and energy and use self-compassion to challenge and reframe these difficult thoughts.

It's difficult to embrace and relax into the moments of your life fully when your happiness is hooked to a future possibility or event. "If I can just lose a few more pounds, then I'll be happy" or "If I can look like her (or him), then my life will be better"—as long as you keep thinking these types of thoughts, you give yourself strong messages that you are not okay now. When these kinds of thoughts motivate you to lose weight, usually they come along with a whip of some kind of self-deprivation or restriction, the next or latest diet. You connect your self-worth to how well you are following the diet and how much weight you lose. When you return to your usual way of eating, you wonder why you gain back the weight you lost, why the diet seemed to work for others but not you. You feel bad and beat yourself up again. You may even eat more, in reaction to the feelings of restriction you had while on the diet.

Self-Kindness Practice to Support Your Intentions

What would it be like to let go of these difficult thoughts? In the present moment, with a mind not attaching to or engaging in these thoughts, you are free and your mind is no longer beating you up. You can put your attention where you choose, including being kind to yourself and others.

1. Notice and label. When you notice these types of discounting thoughts arising about yourself, label them gently as thoughts and shift your attention to the

nourishing breath. Stay with the breath for a few breaths. Allow yourself to rest fully in the space of this present moment.

2. Consider, what are positive, energizing thoughts you can place your attention on? For example, "Feeling healthy and good is important to me," "My body is sacred," "I make healthy choices for myself," "I love and appreciate my life," "How can I make a difference today?"

3. Call upon your overall intentions and the pertinent supportive intentions for each body. Repeat these gently to yourself several times, feeling the kindness, caring, and strength of these words. Use these to empower your life moving forward, taking the next step in this positive framework of compassion and action you are creating.

4. What are the goals you set using SPRIGS? Remind yourself of the concrete steps to achieve your intentions. Recommit to a positive action step that is relevant to this moment.

With this supportive framework you've created you can enjoy the energy that is freed up by letting go of the internal struggle. Enjoy this process and each moment of your life.

With a plan and tools you can focus on how to live your life from a well-nourished place, rather than how to reach a certain weight, or look a certain way, or something else to make everything okay. The greatest gift is that your main struggle (whatever that may be) can come into perspective when you are naturally healthier, happier, and better nourished. It will no longer consume a significant part of your energy and attention, which are now freed up for things that are really important to you. You can rest more happily and peacefully in the present moment held by the supportive framework you've created.

As your struggle, however subtle or strong, decreases, your focus can naturally open up and broaden to include others more fully, without shaming, judging, or envious thoughts. As you judge yourself less, you will also judge others less! You increase your capacity to have fulfilling connections.

Practicing mindfulness doesn't mean all the difficult thoughts will go away, but you have tools so that they no longer take a front seat in your mind. At least they won't stay for very long. By not feeding them with your attention, they will weaken, fade to the background, or simply disappear!

Mindful Presence with Others

A mindful presence is one of the most important ingredients for positive social nourishment. It helps facilitate empathy, compassion, and kindness. Practicing mindfulness and kind, compassionate attention helps you be more present with yourself and others. It is a practice like everything else. Some of us are better at it than others; some of us are naturally more distracted or have a stronger wandering mind than others. Mindfulness is even more important and can make an even greater difference here. When you are with another person and you are having difficulty being present, notice your breath, feel your body. Focus on the person's words, body language, tone of voice. Let them feel your kind, nonjudgmental presence, which is one of the greatest gifts you can give to someone and they can give you. Ask yourself, Am I present enough to connect, to feel empathy, compassion, kindness, humor, lightness, a sense of play or mirth—whatever is called for in the moment? What do I need to adjust to be more present?

You have been practicing the ability to be present with your experience and nourishing your different bodies through day-to-day activities, eating, walking, moving, eliciting nourishing positive emotions, navigating thoughts and feelings, and practicing kindness to yourself and others. You can practice being fully present with others as well. Mindful, kind, compassionate presence is a key way to nourish your social body and others' social bodies!

Mindful Listening. When we practice mindful presence with friends, partners, co-workers, and whomever we meet, we can be fully present to mindfully listen and receive them. You can notice your tendency for the mind to wander, to jump to conclusions, to make assumptions, get distracted easily, and take things personally when they aren't personal. You can come back to the present moment and listen again with an uncluttered mind. You can do this again and again however many times you need to. Listen not only with your ears but with your heart, your eyes, your body, and all your senses. You can reflect back what you heard or highlight the important parts to increase the feeling of being heard.

Mindful Speaking. We speak in many more ways than with our words. Paying attention to the following three components of communication can help you understand the people around you more accurately. It can foster more empathy and compassion and be more congruent with your own communication and speech.

1. ***Body Language:*** Open, friendly postures speak volumes. Hands at the side or engaged in gestures while speaking convey openness, comfort, and friendliness. Crossed arms and contracted body postures convey more of a closed, internal state. It can easily be interpreted as unfriendliness but may be due to discomfort, attempts at comfort, shyness, or managing challenging emotions. Listen between the lines when another is speaking. Simply changing your own body posture to a more open stance when you are speaking can help facilitate greater ease and connection with the receiver. Paying attention to your own breath and centering your attention on your body at first can help ease discomfort or nervousness.

2. ***Voice Expression and Tone:*** Your tone of voice greatly impacts the meaning of words and conveys emotions and your state of mind. It makes the words come alive and delivers the intent. From kind and nurturing, lyrical and light, mellifluous, mean-hearted or sharp, sweet or angry, a landscape and mood are painted with your voice. Studies have shown that even babies are able to tell when an incongruence between seemingly kind or neutral words and hostile intent is conveyed through tone of voice or body language.

3. ***Eye Contact:*** Eyes are beautiful. Eyes are telling. In our culture they are considered the window to the soul. Give whom you are talking to the gift of your eyes. Of course your eyes will glance elsewhere—that is natural, especially when you are retrieving information or reflecting upon a feeling or thought. But see if you can more often than not look at the person you are speaking with. Depending upon your intimacy meter and cultural background, it may feel difficult or easy. Be mindful of the discomfort and be kind with yourself. Keep trying and you may be surprised at how the level of interaction you have with another increases in satisfaction. I sometimes think of Hollywood movies and all the intense gazing that goes on in them. Many of us don't have this level of intensity in real life, but those movies are on to something. Eye contact can make us feel connected, vital, and attuned.

4. ***Words Do Matter:*** Although words themselves are only part of our total communication, they have a strong impact on others. Tone of voice can mediate words somewhat, such as in jokes or teasing. Words can hurt or heal our emotional body and that of others. Our bodies interpret as real what we say to ourselves and can

react with the stress response. They can also react with relaxation and a healing cascade of physiological effects. What we say to others can elicit positive or negative reactions.

With mindfulness you can pause before you speak, particularly when you are emotionally reactive, and consider the impact of your words. You might take a few mindful breaths, come to a space big enough to consider your words, and choose words that are not inflammatory. Choose kindness whenever you can. Words may literally be inflammation-producing in another person's body! You also might choose to engage at a different time when you are calmer or have had some time to get perspective on a situation. No one is perfect, so don't let this be another place to beat yourself up. But with practice this can get easier.

Choose Your Words

When you want to make a request of someone, whether a difficult situation or an easier one, you can follow some tried-and-true steps.

1. Take a mindful pause.
2. Become aware of your feelings, thoughts, and needs around a situation.
3. Find a good time and place to communicate, when you have the other person's full attention and you are both in a relatively calm and resourced place.
4. Use "I" messages rather than "you" messages around how something makes you feel. "You" messages create a blaming tone and put the other person on the defensive. "I" messages allow you to take responsibility for your feelings and keep the line of communication open.
5. Describe the situation in neutral terms: "When _____ happened, I felt _____." Then describe your desired outcome—an action or a compromise.
6. Mindfully listen to the response and negotiate or compromise on a desired outcome.
7. Acknowledge and thank the person for their willingness to listen and try a new outcome.

Here is an example of what your side of the words might look like: "I noticed that at dinner there are often a lot of comments about how much or what I am eating. I feel very self-conscious. Sometimes I notice I feel angry and eat more later, even if I'm not hungry. I'd really appreciate it if you would no longer comment on the amounts that I eat. Would you be willing to try that? Is there anything that could help remind you? Thank you so much for trying. It means a lot to me. I know you really just want to be supportive."

Integrity

People feel safest and trust the most when our words match our intentions. Psychological congruency and safety are important. This includes keeping our word around commitments. Think about the people in your life whom you trust the most and feel closest to. More likely than not, they are the ones you can count on for a supportive phone call or a spontaneous meeting at a café when you need a listening ear or a warm hug. They are the friends that stick by you in hard times, as well as being there for the good. Are you that kind of friend too? If not, consider ways you might increase your own reliability and trustworthiness.

Setting Boundaries

Relationships can be healing, and they can also be toxic. Are there people in your life you always feel bad around? Every relationship needs a tune-up now and then. We can use our skills for good communication and at times may seek professional help, especially for our intimate partnerships and family commitments. But some relationships simply aren't good for you—they can be inflammatory and cause ongoing stress. It can be a relief when you recognize that and begin the process of letting go. Surround yourself with positive, inspiring people to the best of your ability. And use your skills and best intentions to become that kind of person too!

If we all listened fully and deeply to one another, we would have a more peaceful world. If we paid more attention to our words, speech, and the ways we communicate, we could bring more healing and love to others. You can bring these skills of positive social engagement, which nourish both yourself and the larger social body you are part of, to your daily social interactions. The smile you give to another, the hug, the reassuring words, the shared laughter are infectious. That person may turn around and give the same to another, bolstered by your love and caring.

Spread Your Wings

We can have all kinds of relationships that nurture different parts of ourselves. The close confidants—friends to share life events with, whether physically and/or emotionally—are important and can be cultivated and nurtured following the principles outlined above and more. But many other parts of yourself can be fed and nourished in a dynamic social network. What about the friends who meet you intellectually? Whom you share creative pursuits or recreational activities with? Who nourish your emotional body and you theirs? A close confidant may overlap with these, but one person doesn't usually match all the different parts of ourselves.

Becoming part of new communities or more involved in already established communities can broaden and deepen your sense of belonging, engagement, enlivenment. It can improve your mood, health, and your sense of connectedness. And it offers many more opportunities for social support, fun, and fulfilling activities with others when that is what you are really craving, not food! Good, caring friendships might also help motivate you to eat healthier and exercise more through these shared activities and healthy mirroring.

Tips for Expanding Nourishing Relationships

The following tips can help you spread your wings and cultivate more friends and community in your life with similar interests. Some of these suggestions may seem obvious; other ideas may not have occurred to you before.

1. Become more involved in a community you are already part of: your kids' school, community college, university; church or other house of worship; a health or sports club; yoga studio; meet-up groups around a shared interest; performing arts center or museum; community service group; nonprofit organization; environmental or social services; local politics; etc.
2. Look for opportunities to volunteer and attend events that appeal to you.

3. Become involved in a community that is new to you. What are your interests? What have you always wanted to try? Your social support can often increase simply by following your passions and interests.

4. Find this community by asking friends that are involved in activities you are interested in. Scan newspapers, newsletters, bulletins, and local community news publications or search online for events and ways to get involved.

5. Take the initiative. If you're not finding it, create it, on your own or with a friend. Advertise through your social media network, create a meet-up group, offer it through a local organization. Put the word out to your friends. Hold a gathering in a café, at your home, or at a community center.

6. Join a business networking group. Attend professional trainings and learn new skills with others. Become active in your professional organization(s).

7. Choose and maintain social connections and communities that are nourishing. Don't be afraid to let go if you find you are avoiding something you may have outgrown.

Mindful Eating and Social Situations

Social events and eating are often linked, and these events can bring up anxiety and stress. Some people avoid them for fear of going off a particular diet or eating too much of the wrong kinds of food. It's easy to go into mindless eating when we are focused on others and end up feeling overfull. With a few reminders and guidelines you can learn how to increase the nourishment that social connections offer without the pre-event fear, anxiety, or post-event stomach upset or bloat. You can learn how to plan ahead, stay mindful, and enjoy both the food and the company.

Practice in a Variety of Social Situations. Practice the Mindful Check-In. Gently hold your intention and goals in awareness to help navigate your choices. For special occasions, holidays, and celebrations you may want to just have fun, celebrate, and not worry about your choices. Yet there still are ways to enjoy these special events and make choices that enable you to feel good and nourished in your body. For example:

~ *Go to these events no more than moderately hungry; then you can enjoy the food without being blindsided by your stomach. Eat a healthful snack beforehand, so you won't arrive starving and can make better choices.*

~ *See which foods really call to you. Try new tastes and dishes.*

~ *Practice tuning in to your hunger and satiety levels and make your choices accordingly.*

~ *When you've had enough, physically move away from the food tables.*

~ *Hold a partially filled cup or plate as you mingle, if that helps you feel more comfortable. And remember, you don't have to finish the food on your plate just because it's there.*

Stay Mindful While Engaged in Conversation. Daily social eating is a fact of life for most of us. It is possible to enjoy your food, stay attuned, and be social at virtually the same time.

~ *When you eat with others at a sit-down meal or in social situations (meetings, work, holidays, events, celebrations, etc.), practice being present to the conversation.*

~ *Shift your attention to your body and the experience of eating. Notice how good the food tastes, how hungry or satisfied you may be. Let your sensory experience, your chewing and swallowing bring you back fully to eating. Keep your focus here for at least a few seconds.*

~ *Then shift back to the social milieu. Focus on the conversation, mindfully listen, and contribute. Repeat this throughout the meal. Remember the seven tips.*

With practice, you'll become more skilled at remembering to tune in and shift your attention to your body and your eating without letting go of the social conversations and your awareness of the other person(s) occurring in the moment. Having both a formal meditation practice and mindful eating practice can lead to a kind of meta-awareness at times, where you stay aware of and present to conversation and your eating experience at the same time.

Mindful Restaurant Eating. Make this a positive experience for your body. It's easy to eat too much at restaurants or order the kinds of food that do not support your health and well-being. Whether you eat out frequently or as a special treat, these tips can help guide you into more mindful and healthful ordering and eating while still enjoying the whole experience.

~ *Check out menus ahead of time when possible to assess your options.*

~ *Consider forgoing or sharing "extras": appetizers, breads or chips, drinks, desserts. These are easy to eat mindlessly and can leave you unnecessarily full and uncomfortable at the end of a meal. Mindfully savor the ones you do choose.*

~ *Stick with the main meal or even share a dish, depending upon the portion sizes and your hunger levels.*

~ *Ask for sauces and dressings on the side so you control how much is served to your preference.*

~ *Take home what you don't finish once you are satisfied, so it doesn't stay on the table and tempt you.*

~ *Practice the tools of mindful social engagement and mindful eating. Shift your attention away from your conversation periodically to your experience of eating. Savor and enjoy with all your senses. Check into your levels of hunger and fullness and stop when satisfied. Practice meta-awareness.*

Your SPRIGS Goals

Now that you've completed this chapter, consider some specific goals and steps you would like to take to nourish your social body. Put this into the SPRIGS format to help you reach your goals. Revisit, assess how you are doing, and adjust your goals periodically. Write below and/or in your Well Nourished Journal.

_____

_____

_____

_____

OUTER SUPPORT

Consider new ways you can nurture your existing social support. Refer to the tips for expanding nourishing relationships earlier in this chapter. Can you enlist others to join you in potentially casting a wider net of friends? Try new activities together, join a club together, start a new group. Reach out to your social network when you want to support feeding any of your other "bodies." Perhaps you'd like to explore a new hike, try a new yoga class, or go to a new restaurant with a healthy choice menu with a friend. Increase the frequency of your outings with a friend or colleague. Commit to making plans with someone regularly, whether once a week, once a day, or twice a month. Find a fun new activity to share each week from the activity section of the newspaper. Join a work networking group. Create a regular supportive coaching call or meeting with friends or colleagues around shared interests. Gauge your goals with your check-in buddy. Expand your list of nourishing activities to include those that deepen relationships and community. Try at least one new activity in each of the chapters that will also nourish your social connections.

INNER RESOURCES

Bolster yourself with nourishing affirmations and lovingkindness phrases when you set off into new and unknown territory. Use the ALLOWS process (see page 104) to hold any uncomfortable thoughts and feelings (such as insecurity, anxiety) in a field of spacious, kind awareness, lovingkindness, and self-compassion. Use the self-kindness practice to let go of discounting thoughts and empower yourself with energizing thoughts and your intentions. When you feel lonely, whether you have reached out to a friend or not, you can practice self-compassion, hands on your heart, or sitting or walking meditation. Enjoy and savor the good feelings that result. Fill yourself up from the inside. When you rest once again in your vast natural awareness, re-sourced and nourished, loneliness can disappear or be eclipsed by resting in a greater sense of yourself.

Find opportunities to be kind to others: Try smiling at coworkers, people young and old you pass in the streets, at the store, as you go about your errands. Do unexpected little acts of kindness during your day. Pause and take in the other person's appreciation, surprise, or delight. Savor the warm feelings that arise in yourself from these small acts.

Use Your 5 Steps Prompter Tools

[ ] Fill in the social body in your Well Nourished Bowl.

[ ] Fill out your Intention and Goals Prompter for the social body.

[ ] Use your 5 steps Daily Prompter to help support you in mindful choices.

CHAPTER EIGHT

Intellectual Nourishment: Feeding the Mind

When you are fully engaged in your life, feeding your mind in a nourishing way, you are less likely to turn to food for stimulation, diversion, or comfort at those times you aren't really hungry. You can be occupied with the pleasure of an engaged mind, body, and heart.

Intellectual curiosity and engagement are characteristics that make us uniquely human. We feel alive and engaged when we are involved in stimulating pursuits. As we get busier in our lives—lost in our work routines and family responsibilities—it is an area often overlooked. Do you love to learn through classes, books, movies, or conversations? Is your work or volunteering that you do intellectually stimulating? Do you have cultural activities, hobbies, or sports that engage you? Or are you involved in activities that require regular problem solving or complex decision making?

When you are fully engaged in your life, feeding your mind in some way, you are less likely to turn to food for stimulation, diversion, or comfort when you aren't really hungry. Nourishing the intellectual body can give you what you are truly needing, instead of food or another less-than-helpful pastime. So many people eat out of boredom, depression, or anxiety. Instead of being occupied by a vacant or distressed space saying "feed me," you can be occupied with the pleasure of an engaged mind, body, and heart.

What We Know

Intellectual stimulation and growth contribute to greater brain and cognitive health over a lifetime. Intellectual pursuits at any age can lift mood and increase feelings of connection to others through engagement with the community or workplace, cultural involvement, or traditional learning. Intellectual pursuits can involve learning about or participating in the breadth and depth of our world and human experience through different modalities and venues. Cognitive training—including learning new skills, problem solving, making handicrafts, acquiring new information, and reasoning—feeds, maintains, or increases our brain function as we get older.

When your mind is not focused or engaged with the present moment, it naturally wanders. When it is learning something new, being challenged, solving problems, stimulated, you are drawn into the present moment. Research on the wandering mind shows us that the less our minds wander, the more satisfied and happy we are. Thus, the more we are fully engaged in the present moment, the happier we feel. We know that the mind, left to its own devices, wanders to thoughts of the past, the future, to thinking about unfinished business, the list of errands, what's not working. This takes us away from enjoying the moment. So it makes sense that the more fully engaged we are, the quieter our mind is, and the more we rest in the "now." The extraneous flotsam is put to rest for a time.

Novelty and Your Brain

When you are engaged in learning something new, your mind goes into optimal memory enhancement and performance mode. A low level of positive stress hormones, called eustress, can be released. As a result you feel more alive. Your inner critic is silenced as focus increases. Bringing fresh attention to each moment, noticing what is new or different, can add novelty to our daily routine and make life feel more satisfying. Taking little steps to do things differently throughout the day brings this same sense of novelty and aliveness.

Look for ways to increase nourishment to your mind daily, in small or big ways, to bring balance to your eating and your life. It helps to take the focus off food for stimulation and novelty.

In this chapter we'll explore different ways you can feed this part of your life. Sometimes we are in a rut and don't see any new possibilities or feel that anything interests us. But the world is vast, and there is something for everyone, sometimes right in front of your nose. We'll broaden the possibilities if you feel stuck or just simply need a nudge to take the next step.

AWARENESS

○ Pause ○ Reflect ○ Assess

Reflect on the following questions to see which areas of nourishment are lacking or fulfilled in your intellectual body.

~ *Do I regularly engage in intellectual pursuits and mental activities that are stimulating and fulfilling?*

~ *Do I regularly explore new ideas or learn new skills?*

~ *Is lifelong learning important to me?*

~ *Do I engage in personal growth through reading, activities, classes, or from what daily life presents to me?*

If you answered no to any of the questions, you may be hungry for intellectual stimulation and feeding of the intellectual body.

Now make a list of all the topics, subjects, hobbies, and areas in life you have ever been interested in, now and in the past. (There might be some overlap here with your List of Nourishing Activities from chapter 4.) Don't edit as you write. Just jot down everything that comes to mind in the space below and/or your Well Nourished Journal.

I am interested in . . .

_____

_____

_____

Now look at your list. Circle the five that most interest you now.

Mindful Check-In

How does your body feel when you are engaged in intellectual pursuits? Note thoughts, feelings, energy levels, the overall quality of your experience. If it's been a while since you exercised this part of yourself, remember what it felt like when you did. Notice if you have any desires or yearnings for more intellectual engagement now. Do you ever use food to fill an emptiness or void related to lack of intellectual satisfaction or fulfillment?

INTENTION

Create an intention(s) based on your assessment to feed and increase nourishment of your intellectual body. Write these down here or in your Well Nourished Journal.

_____

_____

_____

_____

Write down the top five areas you might want to put your attention on (which you circled above). If your list was short (fewer than five), don't worry. More ideas are coming.

*1.*_____

*2.*_____

*3.*_____

4._____

5._____

Our minds need to be exercised just as much as the rest of our bodies for maintaining and even growing our mental capacity over the years. Intellectual wellness is about learning new things, stretching and challenging the mind. It involves questioning, curiosity, critical thinking, and openness to new ideas.

With mindfulness, we also maintain an open, curious attention to our experience. We let go of preconceptions as we become aware of them and are able to perceive things in a new way. Like intellectual engagement, mindfulness also grows the brain in many positive ways. We can bring mindfulness to our intellectual pursuits, fully awake, aware, and enjoying the gifts and novel challenges that we encounter.

Intellectual pursuits may overlap with the creative body. In our capacity to challenge, to inquire, to question the way things have always been done, we might find our own creative way of eating, living, thinking, and doing. We reflect upon and challenge the status quo of our lives and find new ways of approaching the issues and problems of the day. We may gain new perspectives about history or different cultures in general.

You may be blessed to have work that is already intellectually fulfilling and satisfying. If not, it's all the more reason to make sure this area is well fed.

SKILLS AND TOOLS

There is a variety of ways you can increase intellectual nourishment and engagement in your life; many overlap with emotional, social, and physical fulfillment as well. As we go through these options, really take time to listen to yourself and let the wisdom of your mind, heart, and gut guide you to activities that elicit a big YES from you. As you go through your list and the list of suggestions that follow, be aware of how the "three brains" are responding. Is there a big yes, or a constricting or neutral response? Which of the three centers of wisdom is talking louder? What do your heart and gut say? Is the mind in agreement or creating reasons why you can't do something? If the latter, is that really true for you or is it based on fear, reluctance to move out of your comfort zone, or something else? Use all the body wisdom and information available to guide your choices.

It may be very obvious to you what new things you'd like to bring into your life. Or maybe you are feeling tired, uninspired, and uncertain after years of putting yourself second and not leaving room to nurture your whole self. If you feel overwhelmed and in low spirits, maybe you need to work on the foundations of physical and emotional nourishment first.

Consistent exercise, eating regularly and healthfully for you, getting enough sleep, and practicing meditation and relaxation can make a big difference in your energy and mood. You can draw upon your social support to help lift your spirits and even to share new intellectual pursuits.

I work with so many clients who come to me with full palates but empty palettes. Their lives have become reduced to work, family responsibilities, errands, and few other satisfying activities. Food is the big focus and source of pleasure. When we work on mindful eating concurrent with nourishing the other bodies, the emphasis can begin to shift and our life palette becomes more balanced. The satisfaction that comes from learning, stimulating discourse, new discovery, new communities, and the feelings of engagement from new projects also takes the focus off food and puts it in its rightful place.

Open the Mind

What do you love to do? What did you love to do before you got too busy? If you are an adult, what about when you were a kid? If you're more advanced in age, think back to when you were younger. Follow these simple steps as you read through the following section.

1. ***Brainstorm Your List:*** Look at your list of interests above or in your Well Nourished Journal. If you haven't written one yet, do so now. Remember to let your mind wander, writing down everything that comes to mind without editing. If you've already written it, add any new interests that come to mind.
2. ***What:*** Read through the suggestions in the next section. Circle any that intrigue you and add them to your list here or in your Well Nourished Journal.
3. ***How:*** Read through and circle the learning modalities or activities that you'd like to try. Write them in your Well Nourished Journal.

4. *Choose the two subjects on your list that most interest you.* This can help you to focus on what you'd especially like to explore in your life right now.

5. *Intention:* Make a plan using SPRIGS with specific, doable steps to begin these new intellectual pursuits. Are there times of each day you can devote to these? Morning, afternoon, evenings, before bed? Certain days of the week? Weekends? Make these a regular part of your life.

The ways you can engage in the world that feed your mind are endless. The following suggestions are just a sample of what is possible. They are introduced first by subject, then by different ways to pursue them.

What—Learn as Wide as the World. Were there things you never got to learn about in school or want to explore deeper? History, art, science, health and wellness, environmental health, computers, writing, poetry, travel, literature, philosophy, mindfulness, social media, animal welfare, gardening, culinary arts, puzzles, other languages, religion? Get as specific as you can. Perhaps you're interested in the history of music, a particular branch of science such as geology or astronomy, or a specific genre of literature or author. One easy way to get new ideas or to get inspired is to go to an actual bookstore. As I was writing this chapter, I went into a large bookstore and was delighted by the number of clearly displayed topics and the wide variety of books available. I thought of you, the reader, and what a great way this is besides surfing the Internet to find new topics and go deeper into ones you are already interested in. Take a trip to your local bookstore, grab a cup of tea, and enjoy your new book!

How—Expand Your Exploration. There are so many easily accessible ways to learn these days. Reading books and listening to audio programs are several tried-and-true ways. You can take classes, attend lectures, join discussion and study groups, enroll in a university extension program or community college, participate in community center programs, go to libraries and museums, or engage with a spiritual or religious organization. Learning outside of the home has the added benefits of exposure to new environments and the potential expansion of your social network and community.

You can also stay closer to home and join the online world of learning by participating in live video programs or live or prerecorded webinar courses, entering chat rooms, joining discussion groups, listening to podcasts, watching videos on an endless variety of subjects, or reading social media, newspapers, blogs, and websites in areas you are interested in.

Of course, you can also be the leader and initiate any of these modalities in any subject. Be the one to research, write, or speak about it! Create a course, discussion group, or website in an area you'd like to begin a discourse in. Blog, write articles, write a book! You can advertise groups in a growing number of online event platform websites, in local papers, or at the organizations where you might want to hold your event.

Don't forget about the intellectual nourishment cultural events can offer us. When was the last time you went to see a play, musical, or comedy show? These types of events can engage the mind and expose you to a new world of thoughts, feelings, ideas, and visual and auditory feasts. Look for small, local events as well as the bigger venues.

Nourished through Work

Are you bored or unchallenged with your current job or life circumstance? You might explore ways to make your job more mentally stimulating. Consider studying a new profession, acquiring a new skill set, or finding a different position. Take classes, read, or speak to people who have experience in whatever you're pursuing, or who could offer advice—take them out for a meal, do an informational interview, shadow them for a day at their job. These can be good first steps. Becoming a lay support-group leader or speaking publicly in an area you are passionate about can also be a great start.

Beware of Overstimulation in the Digital Age

Just as we can become overly focused on food, we can become overly focused on the mind. In our quest for ease in the moment, distraction from unpleasant emotions, avoidance of boredom, we often look to stimulate the brain. But what about when we are attempting to do this with electronics? Are you using your smartphone constantly, surfing the Web, texting, or on the computer? It is currently estimated that people are spending more of their daily hours on some form of electronics—whether a smartphone, tablet, or computer—than they are on sleep.

Notice if you are overfeeding the mind with digital activity. Be discerning about the time you spend on your highly addictive devices and what you are focusing on—is it feeding your mind with the best brain food for you? Does it deeply nourish your intellectual body? How much is for work, pleasure, fun, mindful entertainment? How much is just mindless activity? Does it serve your overall intention for health and well-being? Assess how much the time you spend on this part of yourself is in balance with feeding all the different parts of yourself.

As mentioned earlier, when our minds are more focused in the present moment, we can feel more relaxed. Spending time simply being in the moment rejuvenates the mind and intellect. Being outside in nature with no agenda but to appreciate and relax is a great antidote to digital overstimulation.

There can be pitfalls to pursuing intellectual nourishment and related entertainment, whether digital or not. It can disconnect us from ourselves and from tuning in to what we really need in the moment. Are you staying connected to yourself, listening to your body's cues for food and water, the desire for love and connection, friendship, contribution, rest, relaxation, or movement? Maybe you need to nourish one of the other bodies. The key is to stay mindfully present to your experience and balance activity with rest and relaxation. This feeds and rejuvenates the mind as well. On a positive note, maybe more than one body is being nourished at the same time; for example, an intellectual activity can involve movement, social connection, and food. The point is to stay balanced in nourishing all the different parts of yourself, however you shape your unique day and week. When your bowl is full of nourishment, you can be your best self.

Intellectual Support Boosters

The following prompts help you stay balanced, grounded, and feeling good. They will support you with the energy and focus necessary to pursue the mind food that enriches your life and satisfies the human hunger to know, to quest, and to learn. This is an important part of living a well-nourished life and feeling whole.

Eat Food for Brain Power. Include the following in your diet for optimal brain function:

~ *Omega-3 fatty acids:* These improve our brain function and are also good for our heart and joints. Eat two servings a week of high-omega-3 fish, such as salmon, trout, tuna, herring, and sardines. Good vegetarian sources include flaxseeds, *walnuts (also linked to improved mental performance), and some other nuts. You could also take a supplement of fish oils.*

~ ***Berries:*** *Blueberries especially provide a rich source of antioxidants, such as vitamin E, which appears to help our memories.*

~ ***Whole grains:*** *These give a steady supply of B vitamins and slow release of energy to the brain, thus avoiding the potential mood effects and energy swings from the surges and spikes of glucose from processed carbohydrates such as sugar and white flour.*

~ ***Lentils:*** *Offering a good source of the B vitamin folic acid, these are also high in iron, which helps us be more alert.*

~ ***Green leafy and cruciferous vegetables:*** *These veggies are most highly associated with lower levels of cognitive decline. Women who ate plenty of leafy greens and cruciferous veggies in a long-term Harvard study retained their cognitive function, including memory, better than those who ate less.*

~ ***Chocolate:*** *Regular chocolate eaters score significantly higher on cognitive function, including tests on performance, tracking, and memory, as a result of its high concentration of flavonols. Dark chocolate may help protect against aging and dementia. Raw cocoa powder doesn't add as much fat and calories.*

Eating quality food at regular intervals, while honoring your physical hunger, supports a calm, alert mind.

Exercise to Improve Mood and Cognition. Daily exercise improves your intellectual ability and performance. It supports you throughout the day to feel alert and happy; improves your focus, executive functioning, cognition, and memory; and increases positive thinking. You are able to more easily dispel overwhelming feelings that stress can cause and maintain clarity of mind.

Sleep Well. Sufficient sleep gives you the intellectual and creative edge to not just get through the day but to surprise yourself with being your best in all realms of your life. You can use mental space for intellectual pursuits rather than just trying to stay awake.

Meditate and Relax. Relaxation techniques and a regular meditation practice can give you a clearer mind, better focus, and access to new ideas, viewpoints, and inspiration to implement in your life.

Nourishing the intellectual body leads to a sense of wholeness; it honors your unique combination of interests as a human being. It could be said that your interests and passions are a reflection and manifestation of your own blueprint. When you honor these interests and impulses, you are honoring yourself at a very deep level. You are worth it. Now that you are aware and empowered to feed your mind, no need to drown a sense of intellectual unfulfillment or boredom with ice cream or anything else that you don't really need.

Your SPRIGS Goals

Write the specific goals and steps you would like to take to nourish your intellectual body. Put this into the SPRIGS format to help you reach your goals. Revisit, assess how you are doing, and adjust your goals periodically. Write below and/or in your Well Nourished Journal.

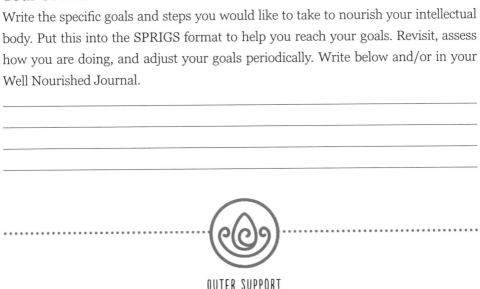

OUTER SUPPORT

Consider all the above suggestions to bolster intellectual nourishment. Try new activities with a friend. Have a stimulating discussion about a shared topic of interest. Reach out to people who might know something about a topic or vocation you're interested in. Expand your network of connections. Invite a new friend from a new activity to tea or a walk to get to know them better. Schedule regular time for your new intellectual pursuits. This includes research and exploration time as well as actually doing the activity. Comb through the activity section of the newspaper. Touch base with your check-in buddy on new or existing goals. Use the SPRIGS process to support your new goals.

INNER RESOURCES

Nourish yourself daily with mindfulness meditation to stay present, replenished, and focused. Practice gratitude, appreciation, and amazement for this unique capacity of your human mind to quest, learn, question, and grow. Deeply acknowledge yourself for the time you take out of your day or week to nourish these interests. Celebrate yourself—your interests, accomplishments, contributions to others, and pursuit of knowledge for its own sake.

Use Your 5 Steps Prompter Tools

[ ] Fill in the intellectual body in your Well Nourished Bowl.

[ ] Fill out your Intention and Goals Prompter for the intellectual body.

[ ] Use your 5 Steps Daily Prompter to help support you in mindful choices.

CHAPTER NINE

Creative Nourishment: Feeding the Soul

A life without creative expression is a life unfulfilled. Let your creativity express through you.

Creativity is a close sister to the intellectual aspects of ourselves. The desire to creatively express is also a uniquely human attribute. When our creative body is regularly nourished, we sense a level of fulfillment and deep satisfaction that may feel as if we're nourishing our soul. When it is not being fed, we may feel an emptiness easily mistaken for food hunger.

The creative body is interrelated with many of the other bodies. Positive moods are actually more powerful predictors of engaging in creative activities than neutral or negative moods, so when the needs of your other bodies, particularly the physical, psychological, and emotional, are being met, you enjoy better overall well-being. Your creative body begins to speak louder to you, and creativity can flow more easily in your life. Creativity can actually feed your emotional body and leave you feeling more peaceful, balanced, and self-expressed. Many people convey their emotions through their art, whether it's visual, performing, or written. They feel better, more alive, and connected throughout the process and afterward.

While nourishing your creative body, you may be feeding your social body too, as many creative pursuits are done in the context of classes or community, or are inspired by collaboration or group work. Learning new information, taking classes, and feeding and stimulating the intellectual body allow for a broader base of knowledge from which the creative process can spring.

You might feel that your creative expression is tied to a sense of purpose or meaning in life. Creativity can go hand in hand with sharing your gifts and talents in the world. The desire to creatively express yourself may come from deep within or may be more connected to fun and play. Your work and creativity might be inseparable, or maybe the way you run your family life is a creative outlet for you. When the creative aspect of your life is not actively expressed, you might feel a sense of restlessness, unfulfillment, a void, or an emptiness, however subtle. These types of feelings can lead to filling up with food, turning to alcohol or drugs, or engaging in other activities in a way that is not nourishing for you ultimately or not giving you what you truly need.

What We Know

When we are involved in being creative, our bodies, mind, and spirit enter a state of absorption sometimes called flow, which is very similar to what we experience with meditation. We are in the timeless present, and with this special focus our thoughts don't wander nearly as much and the judgmental mind and critic are quiet. Flow can be experienced in other highly focused states, but joy and other positive emotions don't necessarily accompany it as they do with the creative process. There are even measurable health benefits, which include a more positive attitude, fewer negative emotions, improvements in the immune system function, and better problem-solving abilities.

The creative process involves many different parts of the brain and neural networks. Creativity is not only engaging in the arts and hobbies, but includes new ways of seeing things, problem solving in original and creative ways, and integrating new and known information to come up with novel ideas and inventions. It helps us be more successful in work and life. Research shows that specific daily activities can increase your creative thinking and abilities. Studies also tell us that those who engage regularly in daily creative activities—drawing, writing, making recipes, or something else—report feeling happier and more active.

You can live your life in creative ways by taking opportunities to do things a little differently throughout the day and following many of the ideas here to foster your own creative lifestyle, expression, and abilities. If you really love food and cooking, food can become the creative activity rather than the problem. The creative process can be enjoyed and the end result of your delicious concoctions savored, eaten, and digested mindfully, joyfully, and fruitfully, rather than mindlessly and fruitlessly.

Everyday creativity can bring more nourishment of the deeper kind into your life. How well is your creative body being nourished?

AWARENESS

○ Pause ○ Reflect ○ Assess

Take a moment now to reflect on the following questions to see which areas of nourishment are lacking or fulfilling in your creative body.

Which of the following statements are true?

~ *I spend time regularly in creative activities that are fulfilling.*

~ *Creative activities are part of my everyday life.*

~ *I stretch myself to learn new skills and ways to express myself creatively.*

~ *I look for creative solutions to problems or challenges.*

~ *I vary my daily and weekly routine and am open to spontaneity.*

If any one of these statements does not ring true for you, you can likely increase nourishment to the creative body. If few of these statements are true for you, then your creative body may be hungry or starving, from a dull ache to large pangs.

Mindful Check-In

What do I notice about my thoughts, feelings, and physical sensations when I am involved in a creative activity or expression? What is the quality of my experience? How often do I experience frustration, sadness, or other difficult emotions from the lack of opportunities for creative expression in my daily life? Do I ever eat from this frustration or engage in unhelpful activities to feel better?

INTENTION

Create an intention based on your inquiry and reflection around nourishment of the creative body. Do you want to increase nourishment in this area or simply support what you are already doing? Consider a specific intention here, and whether you are ready to find, plan for, and schedule fulfilling creative activities on a regular basis. These could include art, dance, music, writing, hobbies, gardening, or whatever brings you joy and fulfillment. Or perhaps there is a way you want to bring more creativity into your work or life as art.

My specific intention for the creative body is:

_____

_____

I would like to explore: (list creative activities)

_____

_____

I would like to incorporate more:

_____

_____

SKILLS AND TOOLS

Resource Yourself

We know that well-being and happiness are fruitful ground for creativity and, conversely, engaging in creativity regularly can also make us happier. Nourishing the first four bodies—physical, emotional, psychological, and social—helps create the foundation to attend to all of your other bodies' needs (intellectual, creative, spiritual, and worldly) and to thrive as a whole person. Meeting your basic needs of food, safety, shelter, and physical health and being able to nurture your emotional and psychological bodies are keys to well-being. Some days you may need to make sure you are more resourced, better nourished in other areas, before being able to fully focus on the creative body. You could enhance your resources in just a few minutes: Check in mindfully. Maybe you need to have a good meal, drink some water, call a friend. Or change things up a bit and go have fun! Take a break, go for a walk, listen to some great music, spend time in nature. Perhaps you can take a nap—sufficient sleep and rest support creativity.

When you engage creatively you step out of the linear mind and list of "to do's" into the creative mind and spirit where anything is possible. The psychologist Abraham Maslow created a hierarchy of needs that must be met for us to reach our full potential. This model is generally represented as a pyramid with the more foundational or basic needs at the bottom: (1) physiological, (2) safety, (3) love and belonging, (4) esteem, and (5) self-actualization at the top. In reality, the hierarchy of these needs may vary for individuals across cultures and may be pursued concurrently. More recently, what we have learned from cross-cultural studies about happiness and fulfillment is that when foundational needs—food, shelter, safety—are met, people report having a good life. Usually these are the needs that people focus on first. But other needs that contribute to well-being and happiness are very important to pursue, even when foundational needs are not being fully met. In fact, daily positive emotions generated from social connection, love, feeling respected and proud of something are very strong predictors of well-being across all the cultures. Although your physical well-being is important in supporting creativity and all the other bodies, this doesn't mean the physical body (and all survival needs) has to be fully resourced first. That isn't always possible. Don't let it be an excuse to not take steps to nourish the other parts of yourself! Your different bodies' needs, such as creativity, can be pursued simultaneously or in an order right for you, based on your personal assessments of your own life. Note where there is the most deficit and where your energy, inspiration, and motivation lie to determine in which order and how much you feed and nurture each of your bodies.

In the cross-cultural study on the hierarchy of needs, positive daily feelings could be experienced even when basic needs were not fully met. This is particularly important to remember because life doesn't always go as planned. The landlord can decide to sell the house, a job can be lost, or with the best of intentions you may have overeaten at a social or work event; but with mindfulness, creativity and creative problem solving, inner resources, social support, and love you, can navigate these changes and even be able to have some measure of well-being throughout.

If you find yourself in challenging circumstances and think creativity isn't necessary, know that it can in fact be a great resource and can lead you back toward taking the struggle off food, helping you find balance and live your whole well-nourished life.

Free Up the Creative Body

Sometimes we resist the creative body. Expressing ourselves creatively can make us feel vulnerable, close to the bones, too exposed. Perhaps you were once judged for a poem, drawing, or piece of artwork that you created. A sense of shame got activated, and the internal critic or inner judge was born around your creative body. You may have had years of being told that your creative passion wasn't important. Perhaps you loved art, dance, or acting as a child, but it wasn't supported by the schools, their budgets, or your parents' values. It's so easy to get shut down in this area, which too often isn't highly valued by our current educational system or culture.

I loved art and theater as a child. In the seventh grade, I chose to focus on academic and college prep courses based on strong family and cultural beliefs and pressures that "you can't make a living" in the arts. I remember the sadness of giving it up and feeling a great soul loss as I focused on more linear and academic pursuits. I was surprised years later, when I read over my elementary school report cards in some forgotten files, that each year contained great accolades about my art. Over the years, I have integrated creative activities into regular parts of my life. These activities offer juice, depth, and soul that I wouldn't trade for anything. I look forward to cultivating more when I am able. Creativity is now a regular part of my work as well. It's never too late to expand creative activities in your life. They can add another dimension of depth, meaning, and enjoyment.

Free Your Creative Body

If you have blocks to freeing your creative body, the following suggestions can help.

1. Recommit to your *daily meditation* practice.
2. Buy or make yourself a journal, separate from your Well Nourished Journal. Write unedited, three days a week or more, whatever comes to you for at least ten to fifteen minutes.
3. Work mindfully to *notice judgment* related to creativity—thoughts such as "I'm not good enough to be creative," "I don't have the time," or "Creativity shouldn't be a priority." When you notice any negative beliefs or shame arising, pause mindfully, take a few breaths, and acknowledge these thoughts and feelings. Choose one or more ways to navigate and transform them (see table).
4. Add an *affirmation* or lovingkindness phrase. Repeat this to yourself after any of these practices when you are in a more open, receptive state. This may help send the kind message to your subconscious even more effectively and bring about positive behavior change.

Mindful Pause	Tool(s) to Navigate and Transform Negative Thoughts or Feelings	Examples of Affirmations
Pause, breathe, and notice discouraging thoughts or feelings.	~ Self-compassion ~ Label and let go of the thought; come back to the present moment. ~ Challenge the thought. ~ Thought breather ~ ALLOWS process (see page 104 in chapter 6) ~ Sitting or walking meditation, yoga, mindful movement ~ Mindful moments (e.g., in the shower, nature, cooking, driving, etc.)	~ My creativity is a source of my power. ~ My creative wellsprings deeply nourish me. ~ Creativity is fun. ~ Creativity is an essential part of my life. ~ Creativity helps me find my way home.
Now focus on the positive thoughts or feelings that are present in your creative body.		

5. Transform challenging *emotions into art*. Use the techniques above to calm yourself and focus. Then draw, paint, write, journal, play music, channel your energy and creativity into a new creation.

6. *Get your creative juices flowing!* Engage in one new creative activity every week: dance in your living room, take a freestyle dance class, sketch, color, write poetry, sing, join a makers' club.

Journaling

Journaling helps you quiet and free the mind and emotions of whatever is bothering you on a given day. It brings you into the present moment, connecting with your own inner wisdom, and improves your feelings of well-being, which sets the stage for creativity.

Studies have shown that journaling lowers stress and anxiety and improves sleep. They indicate that writing in this way for even less than a week can actually improve our immune system function!

Feed Your Soul

Now it's time to integrate some creative activities into your life. These can feel nourishing to the soul as you engage in them, and the positive effects can linger in ways that filling up with food doesn't.

Brainstorm Your List

As we did with intellectual activities, brainstorm all the creative activities you have enjoyed or would like to have as part of your life. Let your mind wander, free-associate, take a few deep breaths. What would fill your soul? What are you missing in your life, however small or big? What did you used to love to do? What have you always wanted to try?

1. Write these activities down without editing the flow of ideas in your Well Nourished Journal.
2. Choose the top three that really call to you.
3. Commit to putting one or more of these into your life on a regular basis using SPRIGS or any goal-setting process.

You can try out different things: dance, art, songwriting, cooking, fashion. You don't have to stick with one. Let your creative body feel nourished. You may find that those true hungers are being met in a way that the extra helping of dessert or bag of chips could never do!

What's Your Creative Outlet?

The possibilities are endless: take a dance class—classical, ethnic, freestyle; join the conscious dance movement; create music; write songs, poetry, fiction, memoir; learn and play an instrument; join a choir, a local theater troupe, an artists' cooperative; engage in classical art, recycled art, hobbies, crafts; volunteer in your child's play or school activities. . . . Need more ideas? Wander a bookstore in the arts or creative section, open any community education brochure, surf the Internet, or use some of the ideas in the previous chapter to help you brainstorm.

Shift Your Perspective

Flexibility of thinking is a hallmark of creativity and mindfulness. Each supports the other. Think about your whole life and all the things you do each day from different aspects of your life—family, work, social, creative, intellectual involvement, hobbies, community involvement, and pet care. Write them down if you wish.

How much of this are you truly present for? Appreciating fully? How much of the time are you worrying or thinking about food, your body image, or other concerns of the day instead? Does it seem like it's most of the day or a huge part of your day? This is not uncommon for those struggling with food or other issues.

Open up to a bigger perspective. Take a step back and consider all you have to be grateful for and the richness and nourishment of your life that you are building. Fill yourself with gratitude and appreciation in this moment rather than focusing on worries and judgment.

Next time you notice your thoughts and feelings going in the direction of worry and preoccupation, bring yourself out of the trance of your thoughts. Take notice of the moment and what you are actually doing. Can you bring yourself back to the present and savor what is there? If you cannot find much to celebrate, think about what you do have to be grateful for in this miracle of life.

With less energy going toward struggle, the creative body has more of a chance to emerge. In this space you have created, new ways of seeing or doing things may arise. You can even choose to live your life as art.

Being Time, Beginner's Mind, and Creativity

Make sure you give yourself time to just be, "being time." When was the last time you lay in a hammock or sat in the garden? Or just sipped a cup of tea while soaking in the morning sunshine? Being time helps to rejuvenate, get in touch with inner wisdom, and come back more creatively refreshed and renewed.

Spend time savoring your surroundings with all your senses, particularly when you are in a new, inspiring, supportive, or beautiful environment or nature. Leave behind the judgmental mind and any preconceived ideas about what you are noticing. This helps cultivate beginner's mind—a fresh approach to the moment where everything feels new and vivid. Such fertile ground allows for new ways of seeing things and experiencing a greater sense of yourself as a creative being connected to all of life and its possibilities. New associations and connections in the brain occur.

Make Your Life Art

Why choose to approach your life as art? It can get you out of your dry or usual routines and into a way of living that is alive, vital, creative, and fun. Paint your life using your own unique palette of activities.

Turn Life into Art

1. Vary your routine in big or little ways to the extent you can.
2. Buy some fun new jewelry or a pretty hat; express yourself through your clothing.
3. Put your unique stamp on your life—the way you eat, cook, do your schedule.
4. Try new recipes, new vegetables, and ethnic foods. Savor them mindfully.
5. Beautify your environment in your home, office, and garden. Change things up seasonally or annually. Rearrange pictures and wall hangings or buy some new ones. Add fresh flowers.
6. Post inspiring quotes around you from authors, musicians, poets, artists, anyone involved wholeheartedly in creative endeavors.
7. Plan regular creativity playdates with yourself or a friend; it can be a prearranged activity or spontaneous and flexible time to simply follow your nose.

8. Approach life with a sense of adventure, play, and curiosity.

9. Organize creative salons with friends or other invited guests at your home or community venue. Choose a theme such as music or poetry.

10. Join a craft night or creativity circle with friends. Share social time and/or quiet focused time together.

11. Go on creative, spontaneous adventures with your family, friends, or just yourself. Even a trip to the coffee shop could lead to an interesting conversation with someone.

Let the mystery and rewards of the creative life evolve. There is only so much we can plan for. When the creative body is well fed and expressed, you may experience more flow, satisfaction, synchronicity, and joy in your life.

Ten Ways to Increase Creative Thinking and Living

Creativity researchers have found that creative thinking and living can be trainable. You can implement activities into your life that lead to fresh new ideas and stir your creative juices and ways of living. Many overlap with nurturing your social and intellectual bodies.

1. ***Capture new ideas in the moment.*** Take notes in a notepad, on a tablet or smartphone, or email them to yourself. Record ideas into a voice recorder or smartphone. New ideas are often generated when the mind is relaxed, wandering, or in a meditative state. The moments between sleep and waking, while taking a shower, being out in nature, taking a walk, meditating, daydreaming, or conversing are all times when creative, new, and spontaneous ideas can arise.

2. ***Challenge yourself.*** Take on new tasks or endeavors that you wouldn't usually do. Try new puzzles or problem solve difficult tasks, even those that don't necessarily have a solution—anything that challenges you and moves you out of your comfort zone.

3. ***Enhance and broaden your knowledge.*** Seek knowledge and skills that are outside your areas of expertise. Take classes, read about new subjects, peruse

a library or bookstore for ideas and materials, surf the Internet to expand your knowledge. Pick a subject you've always wanted to learn more about or just follow your nose. Broadening your knowledge helps your brain to have more dots to connect to come up with those new creative ideas.

4. **Enrich your environment.** Seek out new stimulation and activities in your life. Listen to new types of music; attend concerts or theater or dance performances; go to events, throw dinner parties, and volunteer in organizations that will surround you with diverse and interesting people. Strike up a conversation with the person sitting next to you while you are traveling. You never know what interesting commonalities you'll find, or new experiences and ideas that may be generated. Rearranging or changing up your immediate work or home environment regularly can also stimulate creativity and feelings of novelty. A peaceful, beautiful environment contributes to feelings of well-being and happiness, which is fruitful ground for creativity.

5. **Reduce screen time.** The amount of time you spend on the screen is time taken away from engaging directly with your creative activities and with others that can stimulate creativity too. Unless of course you are using the screen in service to creativity—writing, learning about new things, creating art, composing music, and so on.

6. **Problem solve in novel ways.** Identify a problem or issue in your life that can be solvable in some way. Get into a relaxed, resourced state and brainstorm solutions. Write out pros and cons and note which solution has more pros. You have used your mind; now look at the list and listen to your heart and gut. Which solution resonates and is most aligned with your "three centers of wisdom or brains" (see page 114 in chapter 6)?

7. **Practice self-care.** Get a good night's sleep the day before a particularly creative task. Take a nap if you need to. Go for a walk or do some other physical activity before engaging.

8. **Eat well.** Choose to eat a balanced meal intentionally to support the mind and creative process. Eat to no more than moderate fullness to optimize your alertness and comfort. Include food boosters for brain power from chapter 8 and foods high in tyrosine, such as bananas, peaches, and almonds, which has been found to increase creative problem-solving abilities.

9. ***Practice mindful moments and meditate.*** Spend time mindfully in the numinous mystery of the moment where conceptions, rules, and beliefs are suspended. The mind is quiet and the world more vivid. Meditate, contemplate, spend time in awe. Let the birth of new ideas emerge from the mystery and space that is opened up in this freedom.

10. ***Just do it.*** Don't procrastinate—just commit to your creative project. Put the time on your calendar, make it a nonnegotiable, precious appointment with yourself.

Make Time

By this point in the book, some of you may be wondering how you can make time to nourish your creative, intellectual, social, physical, emotional, and psychological bodies, carry on your daily work and/or family responsibilities, and have a regular practice of mindfulness meditation. And I ask, how can you not?! With an open, flexible mind, which is part of the traits of creativity, you can find ways to make all these important parts of yourself a priority. Some of these ways don't really take extra time but are a new way of being and working mindfully with what arises. With approximately sixteen to eighteen waking hours every day, and hopefully a weekend or other days off from major responsibilities, you have the time to craft a vibrant, fulfilled life where you can be your best, healthiest self and a caring, contributing member to your community. How this works for you now may not apply in a different life stage (depending on family, work, retirement) or for someone else. Embrace your life as it unfolds, celebrate it, and set your comparing mind aside. The well-nourished creative body will add a particular flavor and zest that is deeply life affirming.

Your SPRIGS Goals

In your Well Nourished Journal and/or in the spaces below, write down all the steps you feel inspired to take to nourish your creative body. Put those that feel more difficult into the SPRIGS goal format as you'd like.

_____

_____

_____

_____

OUTER SUPPORT

Engaging in creative activities can seem more doable and even more exciting when you reach out to others who might share your interests and passions. You can feed your social body as you nourish your creative self—perhaps you take dance classes, join a theater community, or collaborate with fellow artists on an exhibition. Touch base with your check-in buddy; perhaps you would like to pursue the same creative goals together. Find outer support independently as well. Get inspired by visiting art museums or reading about great artists. Watch for exhibits or performances in local listings. Listen to inspiring, uplifting, and beautiful music. Beautify your environment, fill your space with art or objects that move you, display your own creations, make art out of quotes, or post them around your home or office. Limit screen time and keep your physical body healthy with exercise to help spur creativity. Spend some time in nature to get inspired. Check in with your check-in buddy on new steps and goals. You might also use the SPRIGS process to support your new goals.

INNER RESOURCES

Meditation and mindfulness will help you free any blocks in your creative body. With self-compassion, notice the negative thoughts you might have about your creativity and work with them, which will allow you to better express yourself. Practice gratitude and appreciation for the freshness, mystery, and unpredictability of your creative endeavors. Savor the process and outcomes. Deeply acknowledge yourself for the time you open up to commit to these interests, activities, and new ways of approaching your life. You are worth it. Celebrate yourself and how your unique creative spirit manifests. When it touches or inspires others, take that in.

Use Your 5 Steps Prompter Tools

[ ] Fill in the creative body in your Well Nourished Bowl.

[ ] Fill out your Intention and Goals Prompter for the creative body.

[ ] Use your 5 Steps Daily Prompter to help support you in mindful choices.

CHAPTER TEN

Spiritual Nourishment: Sourcing Your Deeper Connection

When you are connected to the deeper nourishment, the wanting, the needing something else to be okay seems to fall away. You feel full in the most positive, joyful, and spacious sense.

Does your sense of something greater than yourself help you access feelings of peace, joy, and awe, a sense of rightness or harmony in your life, regularly? Do you have practices, routines, or activities that help nurture this important part of you? Is your sense of spirituality connected to a community, to nature, or does it come from more solitary moments communing with the divine? Welcome to the numinous, mysterious, heartful, vast, and boundless aspect of ourselves we call spirituality. Nourishing this often underrecognized body is integral to our well-being.

Some of us seem to come into the world naturally connected to spirituality, having a deep knowing of something beyond what exists in the known physical world around us. Others discover this innate sense along the life cycle, in times of difficulty, in the temple of nature, in dance, during life transitions, or through inspirational teachings and religious experiences. Great religions have been built around this shared desire to connect with something greater than ourselves. Spirituality can give us meaning, purpose, and desire to be of service beyond the sphere of our own self. We feel love, compassion, peace, equanimity, and kindness.

Whatever you may call this sense—God, the Universe, Higher Power, Source, the Divine, the One, the Beloved—and whatever your beliefs are, it is precious and real to you. When you are full and connected to your spiritual body—resting in deep peace, expansive joy, exquisite stillness—insatiable hungers for more material things, approval, or recognition simply disappear. Of course we have human bodies with very real needs (food, water, shelter, and social connection), but our cravings and desires subside for things that ultimately aren't primary for our survival. Instead, from this place of fullness, our essential needs can speak to us clearly.

You don't have to go to a monastery or spend years on retreat to begin to experience these moments. Think about how you felt the last time you came out of a wonderful yoga class, your body vibrating with well-being and your mind clear, or the stillness and contentment after meditation or prayer. What about a beautiful, rejuvenating hike in nature? Whatever you do next, whatever actions you take, are much more likely to be kind and uplifting to yourself or another. That tub of ice cream stays in the freezer. Harsh words barely form in your mind when someone accidentally bumps into you. You make the nourishing choice.

Reclaim the Spiritual

This spiritual sense of yourself, and the qualities associated with it, has not been particularly validated or recognized in our mass-produced, capitalistic culture. So many things draw our attention outside of ourselves, from negative news, consumerism, striving to look and dress a certain way, driven by demanding career goals, suffering from internalized messages that we must be a certain way to be a worthwhile person. Even being a mother these days can be fraught with comparison and competition from who is doing it better and providing her child with more opportunities. We can be consumed by a comparing mind, not feeling good enough, and focusing on external measures of personal goodness and worth.

The quest for thinness has been elevated almost to that of a religion for many individuals. With the huge emphasis in this culture on a particular body shape and size as a key to happiness, you may find yourself spending an inordinate amount of time focusing on achieving the perfect weight. You may follow food rules and practices to adhere to a particular diet and feel bad when you don't measure up (or down). This self-judgment may lead to a backlash and overeating or just a general feeling that you are "not okay." This quest for a thin body is often a desire to deepen your sense of self-worth and acceptance in the eyes of yourself and others. It hijacks the energy that could be used to follow a more authentic and deeply satisfying life, with a focus on deeper values, universally positive qualities, wellness for health's sake, and service to others. Consider the possibilities if you could free up this energy and drop into your wellsprings again and again, sourcing your deeper connection.

No need to blame yourself. The cultural forces are strong. There are few mirrors directed at you in mainstream culture and media reflecting, recognizing, and valuing the sacred and your spiritual body, or celebrating the variety of shapes and sizes that we are. Yet it's this inner and outer quest for the sacred that can offer us the deeper peace. What if you spent a small part of your day cultivating a sense of the sacred, of awe, of connecting to the place of peace that exists inside of you? This sense of the sacred from attending to your spiritual body begins to extend to all aspects of your life if you allow it to, including your physical body.

The body you inhabit is sacred. It is made up of the same elements found in the earth and sky; in fact, the vast majority of your body is actually composed of water. It is just as worthy of being protected and kept healthy and safe as our one planet Earth is.

Body Beautiful

Cultural views of beauty and "acceptable" body types vary greatly across the globe and throughout history. Did you know thousands of statuettes of the female form have been found around the world, dating as far back as 25,000 to 30,000 years? These female figurines are of all shapes and sizes and suggest a celebration and reverence of the Feminine to the stature of Goddess. Some of these figurines were quite ample, such as the so-called Venus of Willendorf. During the Renaissance and in Baroque times, women's bodies were painted much fuller than today, reflecting their contemporary standards of beauty.

What would it be like to let go of the culturally bound ideas of the ideal body and accept your body type as it is? To acknowledge and celebrate your beauty from the inside out? To eat and live mindfully and healthfully from a place of fullness and care because you want to live a well-nourished life? Then you can truly be a happy, joyful contributing member of your local and global communities. You can stop the struggle and make choices based on achieving your highest potential and health rather than based on feelings of deficit.

So how do you learn to pay attention to the abundant source of goodness that you are? How do you give your comparing mind and striving a rest and turn attention back inside? This chapter explores ways to keep your spiritual connection alive and vibrant and a source of nourishment that you can return to again and again. Whether your predilection is to be an everyday mystic full of the Divine or just to find a simple sense of peace and freedom from preoccupation with food, your body, and other worries, you can find some things here to help you on this journey.

What We Know

Research suggests that those who have spiritual beliefs and/or practices live longer, have a more positive outlook, and enjoy a better quality of life. Being regularly connected to a community may also be part of this. We know that those who meditate regularly have a greater sense of spiritual connection and feelings of awe, which are linked to better health and social engagement, and a direct connection to nonconceptual experience as the mind quiets. Meditation has been found to support those in recovery from addiction as part of a sustainable treatment program.

Spirituality is very personal. You may feel you are not a spiritual person, but you likely have things in your life that you connect to and that give you a sense of meaning and purpose. Perhaps in that moment in a sports game when thousands of people are cheering for the same team, a sense of unified purpose, oneness, or awe overtakes you. You may have experienced this at a rock concert when the notes of an old favorite ring out and a thrill runs through the crowd, as everyone gets to their feet and sings along. You are part of a magnificent experience of unity in that moment. You can cultivate and deepen your sense of spirituality, whatever that may be for you.

AWARENESS

○ Pause ○ Reflect ○ Assess

How true are the following statements?

~ *I feel connected to something greater than myself that I can turn to for solace, comfort, connection, or inspiration (e.g., God, Higher Self, Spirit, Universe, Nature).*

~ *I feel a sense of meaning and purpose in my life.*

~ *The little things don't bother me too much because I am grateful to be here in this miracle called life.*

~ *I spend time regularly appreciating nature.*

~ *I contribute to a "cause" or work that is linked to making the world a better place.*

~ *I am part of a community that shares the same spiritual values or beliefs as myself.*

~ *I have a sense of trust that everything will work out okay.*

If you answered no to some of these questions, you may benefit by paying more attention to your spiritual body.

Mindful Check-In

What do I notice in my mind, body, heart, and spirit when I am feeling spiritually connected? What helps me feel connected, stay connected? What are the causes and circumstances that lead to feelings of peace, joy, or balance? Do I ever eat in the moments of not feeling connected? Out of feelings of emptiness? How do I get myself back to balance?

INTENTION

Create an intention(s) based on your inquiry and reflection around nourishment of the spiritual body. Do you want to bring more awareness to this part of your life? Do you want to develop more opportunities or practices in your life to nourish the spiritual body? Write it down below and/or in your Well Nourished Journal.

_____

_____

_____

SKILLS AND TOOLS

We can cultivate three components of spirituality: (1) a sense of something greater than ourselves, (2) a sense of awe, and (3) a sense of meaning or purpose. Regular ways of connecting to spirituality can be found in the continuum of our daily life experience, through everyday spirituality, in community, or through personal times of meditation, dance, or prayer. We'll explore in particular ways to cultivate the first two in this section: how to feel connected to something greater and experiencing awe. (How we bring personal sense of meaning and purpose into our contributions to the world is the main focus for the next chapter.)

Mindful Spirituality

Everyday mindfulness helps us enter the world of nonconceptual reality, where everything is fresh and new. In this space we are more apt to connect to a deeper sense of wonder and awe. We can practice mindfulness while eating our food, taking a walk, or in any everyday activity. A regular meditation practice opens you up to experiences of vastness, joy, love, and peace within and lessens your identification with everyday cares, worries, and stress. Over time you become more grounded in this bigger experience of yourself as pure, buoyant awareness. You can come back to that more easily throughout the day, through a mindful breath, in the spaces in between your thoughts. This space may not open you to the greater mystery and sense of something bigger than yourself at all times, but the invitation and doorway are always open through entering into the now.

Full of Awe

Awe is a particular experience associated with spirituality, a sense of reverence and wonder that transcends and expands our usual perspective on the world. Awe can occur in daily moments enjoying beauty, nature, or art or being moved by acts of kindness and altruism by others. Studies show that experiences of awe are connected with greater health and well-being, even just a few weeks later, and can increase altruism. Awe helps calm the inflammatory response that is responsible for chronic diseases and increased susceptibility to illnesses. It reduces proinflammatory cytokines, substances secreted by certain immune cells, more significantly than any other positive emotion. In a worldwide survey, awe was reported most commonly experienced with birth, death, altruism, and in nature.

Think about how you can increase your daily diet of awe: read positive news about who's making a difference in the world; get out into nature even if it's just stepping outside for a few moments in the middle of a workday; take in the sunshine and the miracle of the flowers or birdsong greeting you outside. Drink in the gift of the colors, textures, and variety of the food you eat. Let yourself be inspired by those pushing the edge of human potential and challenging the status quo by creating new works of art or achieving new milestones in performance or sports. Receive the gifts that come from living with this attention, appreciation, and awareness. You never know when those feelings of interconnectedness and that sense of something beyond your self, even the sense of sacred, may flood in.

In the Cathedral

Where is your cathedral? It might be a physical place, a community place of worship. It might be in your heart. It might be in the cathedral of nature—the grove of old-growth redwoods or stand of evergreen trees just outside your town, or the expanse of wild sea and rocky shoreline that extends for miles just beyond your neighborhood. It could be found in the eyes of all those you serve at a homeless shelter or pop-up soup kitchen in the city—our common humanity reflected back to you, lifted up and supported by your loving hands and caring heart.

Plan regular visits to the places, community, and friends that nourish your spirit and bring perspective. Visit your cathedrals regularly for inspiration and support. We can't always be in the physical locations that bring us home to ourselves, or be with the communities that support this, but we can easily visit our heart and come back to our breath. Use the daily practices suggested here to uplift your heart, mind, and body.

The Wonder of Nature

Nature is a universal cathedral, a temple where many of us find great peace, our first feelings of spirituality, our home. Nature is free of imposed beliefs, of human-made culture and things. In nature we can find a great sense of peace and well-being. An abundance of research now shows how spending even a little bit of time in nature each day can lead to dramatic improvements in physical and mental health and happiness. If you grew up in a city and didn't have much daily exposure to nature from the surrounding countryside or parks, it may feel a little foreign to you or even uncomfortable to spend much time in open land, camping, or walking by the ocean or lake. You can start out with just small amounts of time. Go out with a friend or a guide such as a naturalist, park ranger, or ecotherapist to get comfortable. Consider a tour or planned hike, then linger behind to enjoy the silence and direct connection to the nature around you. This nourishing activity could help quell a misdirected desire to eat.

Practice Heartfulness

While grace can open the door at any moment of your life, regular practices are so important. They help open you to your spiritual body and regularly connect thereafter. The door can be kept open wide, even if only a crack at times, by attention, intention, and practices. Sometimes all you may feel is the warmth and glow of love on the other side of the door, not connected to any particular thing or person.

When you know this place, you don't need to search blindly outside of yourself for meaning. The world becomes a place that you want to honor and take care of. You naturally want to take care of yourself too and to share your gifts. You have a part in this unfolding. But life can get in the way, and you can forget to nurture the spiritual body. Mindfulness and daily practices are so key to support the continued unfolding.

We often experience the world through our head, overlaid with thinking about everything we see, evaluating, making judgments, plans, and lists, comparing what we see in this moment to a previous experience. With just a subtle shift of perspective we can bring our awareness from our head to our heart and meet the world from there. This is a way to become present and spacious. Our heart is vast as our awareness is vast. Practice having an open, resonant, loving heart, positively affecting all those around you and fostering greater connection with them. That sense of interconnectedness is part of spiritual experience. Sometimes you feel vulnerable leading with an open heart. Honor what is true for you in the moment yet don't be afraid to take risks. Heartfulness can be an aspiration, and lovingkindness practices can help guide us back to a heart full of compassion, love, and kindness.

Twelve Suggested Daily Spiritual Practices

Establish daily routines for foundational practices and allow spontaneity for other practices.

1. First thing in the morning, say hello to your spiritual body with your eyes closed. Simply rest in awareness of your body, do a body scan, or rest in awareness of your heart. Bring to mind what you are grateful for, or simply appreciate this moment of stillness and being.
2. Gaze at the mirror, look yourself in the eyes, and take in your inner beauty. Appreciate that you are a spiritual being.
3. Practice mindfulness meditation, lovingkindness meditation, mindful movement such as yoga, qi gong, tai chi, or mindful walking. Plan for a regular daily time to practice, with other options if you miss it.
4. Journal after your practices or at other times of the day.
5. Eat at least one meal mindfully a day, appreciating the wonder of your food, the potpourri of senses and the gift of nourishment the food brings to start your day. Begin to expand this to all meals and snacks, creating ways and cues to remember.

6.	Practice mindfulness of everyday activities with the intention to appreciate, with all your senses, the miracle that you are here, this miracle of life, doing whatever you are doing.

7.	Practice mindfulness of being. Take time in your day to be still: Listen to the birds or wind through the trees; rest on that comfy overstuffed living room chair and take in the room around you; appreciate the view outside your window; sip a cup of tea, contemplating stillness.

8.	Be in nature, receiving the beauty, simplicity, and natural order around you. Contemplate the miracle. Feel your intrinsic belonging in it and the ground beneath your feet. Stand, sit, lie down, walk, roll down a grassy hill or a sand dune! Practice "receiving the gift" (see chapter 5).

9.	Gaze at something beautiful, such as an object in nature or a work of art—the Japanese maple outside your window, the special glass-blown vase, your cat. Take in the gifts.

10.	Gaze at something awe-inspiring—a beautiful sunset, majestic mountain range, towering verdant trees, special architecture, works of art, a rainbow, a crescent moon, a starry sky.

11.	Appreciate the sacredness of what you see around you, of your body, of others and of our planet Earth. Practice kindness toward all.

12.	Give back to the world in some way that reflects your spiritual values and sense of purpose, sourcing your deeper connection.

Weekly or Monthly Spiritual Practices

Add putting not only daily practices but weekly or monthly activities into your life.

~ *Attend religious or spiritual services, circles, meditation classes or retreats.*

~ *Join yoga or other movement classes, singing groups, conscious dance classes or events.*

~ *Design your own weekly or monthly day of practice.*

~ *Volunteer or offer service in your community—the social aspect benefits our health and our spiritual bodies and enhances our connections.*

~ *Find a local group for any of these or join an online group. Or create one of your own in your community.*

Awakening on a Mountaintop: A Personal Story

When I was seventeen years old, on the last day of a backpack trip, I climbed up to the top of a mountain in the Sierras. Comfortably seated at the summit, with an incredible panoramic view, my perception and experience suddenly shifted profoundly. The world opened to me as a numinous, sacred, alive place of incredible beauty and harmony. I experienced everything as in perfect balance and order. The peace was profound, and the vast yet deep, interconnected nature of all of reality became clear. (Some might call this a religious or mystical experience.) I knew at that moment that whatever I did with my life, it needed to be in service to helping others know and access this place. A deep sense of purpose was born at that moment, connected to the desire to serve.

During that revelation on the mountaintop, I knew in a flash what the great mystics, poets, and artists were trying to communicate. I didn't know what my medium would be at that time, but my purpose in life to help bring this knowing to others became a clear guiding light that has always lit my way. That path continues to unfold with teaching, speaking, and working individually with people from all over the world. For all, I am grateful, including the opportunity to share further with this book. I was forever changed by that experience, and my meditation, spiritual practices, and daily connection keep this alive.

Your SPRIGS Goals

Write down all the new daily practices you'd like to incorporate to nourish your spiritual body here and/or in your Well Nourished Journal. Put ones that are new or feel more difficult into the SPRIGS format if you'd like. Make daily reminders for your plan—put them on your calendar, in your phone, leave notes for yourself.

_____

_____

_____

OUTER SUPPORT

Create the support you need so you are not just a human doing but a human being each day. Plan for downtimes, moments to appreciate the sacred. Ask for help and delegate work or home duties when you can. Join a group or center that supports and shares your particular predilection to spirituality. Find and attend a mindfulness meditation group or mindfulness yoga class with a friend or buddy. Plan your workday around these and all nourishing activities when you can, rather than the other way around. Attend a mindfulness retreat at least once a year. If you are interested in exploring organized religion, ask to go along with a friend to their house of worship.

INNER RESOURCES

Practice the daily spiritual practices to nourish your spiritual body. Plan your day so you have ample opportunities to rest in your heart and settle your attention on awe-inspiring moments, however little or big, with gratitude and appreciation of the moment. Spend time in the cathedral of nature. When you feel the urge to eat, take a Mindful Check-In. Am I truly hungry? Is this a meal or snack time? What do I really need right now? Have I fed my spiritual body today? This week? What do I need to plan for now or later today to nourish this often neglected body?

Use Your 5 Steps Prompter Tools

[ ] Fill in the spiritual body in your Well Nourished Bowl.

[ ] Fill out your Intention and Goals Prompter for the spiritual body.

[ ] Use your 5 Steps Daily Prompter to help support you in mindful choices.

CHAPTER ELEVEN

Worldly Nourishment: Embodying Your Unique Purpose and Contribution

May my words, thoughts, and actions today contribute to the happiness, freedom, and peace of all beings. May all be happy, may all be peaceful, may all be free, may no one know suffering on my account or that of any others.

At this point in the book, you may feel that your bowl is much fuller than when you first began to read. You may have earnestly answered the mindful assessment questions in each chapter, reflected on what really matters to you and what's missing in your life, and begun making the small, doable changes to bring about more balance and fulfillment. You may be practicing more mindfulness with your eating and living, through sitting meditation, mindfully pausing, and using many of the tools and practices to support these changes. A focus on food that may have felt out of balance for you is slowly shifting toward eating for nourishment and well-being in quantities and ways that don't harm. You are finding many new ways to nourish yourself.

Now that your bowl is fuller, you can turn your attention out into the world from a much more resourced place. Giving to others, making a difference, is deeply satisfying, especially when you find and engage regularly in ways that are meaningful to you and maximize your unique gifts. Living life with a sense of purpose and making a positive difference in the world in accordance with your values is one of the deepest, most enduring sources of nourishment. You might have stumbled upon your sense of purpose by living your life fully and actively engaging with all the parts of yourself. Or you might have a deep sense of purpose from a young age. It might feel like a light has gone on inside of you that burns steady, high, or low throughout the different circumstances of your life. Your sense of purpose might feel connected to creativity or spirituality, social or environmental causes. When it brings you out of your individual self to feel the interconnectedness with all things, you may experience a natural desire to serve, using your gifts to help to make the world a better place.

Meet your worldly body, most alive and healthy when engaged with the world in positive ways.

In a very real way, we are all interconnected, whether we are aware of that on a daily basis or not. When we feel that sense of interconnection through mindful moments, embodying our purpose, engaging in service, our mood is brighter, we rest easier, and the sense of our small, isolated self dissolves. These moments come easier when we are involved in causes and work with others toward common goals we deeply believe in. They might come unexpected and unbidden as a moment of grace, even experienced as awe as we live our lives.

Our lives can be so stressful, either overly busy or with a sudden vacant space created by a recent job loss, retirement, or breakup. At night after all the day's activities and evening meal are done, in the midst of working, tending to children, or studying for an exam or after the long stretch of an unplanned day, we may have moments where we feel separate and isolated from others. Feeling lonely and isolated can lead to a depressed mood. It can be exacerbated when we don't have a sense of purpose or have lost our way. Our daily activities become rote and we go through them without joy and zest. Food can become a temporary solace, a salve for what we don't have. Think if you could instead connect to your sense of purpose or contribute in some way, however small, that day or evening. The nourishment from this connection can help carry you during those momentary periods of feeling alone and separate and brings you back to a sense of belonging. You know that you have your own unique combination of gifts to share, and this keeps you going.

An authentic sense of purpose that is deeply satisfying almost always involves a measure of inspiring others, service, and contribution. We usually feel quite passionate about it or at the very least care deeply. If none of this rings true for you right now, you might look a little deeper. See if your sense of purpose, or what you think it might be, is truly coming from the deepest parts of yourself, from a passion, from your heart. Or is it coming instead from "shoulds," what you think you should be doing?

Have you been trying to follow greater cultural or family messages that don't apply to your deepest self, letting them define who you are and what you should be doing? Are you living a life of plain pasta and forgoing the pesto or wild mushroom sauce? You can have your pasta and your tasty sauce. If you are struggling to find a new sense of purpose that fits with what you are passionate about, what you really care about, and what might match the unique gifts you bring, you can begin to change that now. Living your purpose may mean making some slight adjustments or it may mean changing the way you live your life more dramatically.

As you've begun to explore nourishing your physical, emotional, psychological, social, intellectual, creative, and spiritual bodies, you may already have discovered some new passions or sense of purpose, including making a difference in the world. Your bodies may support each other and interrelate in fun, and unexpected, ways to this end. As you become full in all these ways, the focus on food can begin to let up.

What We Know

Cross-cultural studies show that being connected socially is correlated with the strongest sense of happiness and life satisfaction. A large body of research shows us that engaging in altruistic behavior, helping others with no specific gain for ourselves, improves our level of health and happiness significantly. Those that have a strong sense of purpose live longer. We thrive when we're involved in helping each other and our planet.

A classic study done in a nursing home community showed that those with a plant to care for and water, lived longer. People with hospital rooms that looked out on nature recovered from surgery faster than those who didn't. And hospital gardens had positive healing effects for those who spent time in them. Being in nature for as little as ten minutes daily can have a significant impact on our well-being. Loving and caring for your pets decrease anger and anxiety, increase happiness, and improve cardiovascular health. Walking your dog gets you out to meet people more. Nature, pets, each other are all integral parts of life we take for granted. They are fundamental to our health and happiness. Yet all of this only thrives with a healthy planet. Taking care of our planet is integral to supporting all life as we know it. Against this broad landscape of our world, your part is beckoning to you like a sparkling dewdrop.

You don't have to carry the world on your shoulders; there are billions of us, each playing our small part, each with unique colors and hues, like shining jewels. Some of you will have larger parts than others. What is yours? If you are reading this book, you likely have more tangible resources than so many others around the world who are less fortunate, often with less equality and freedom as well. Whatever role you play, it's significant. Kindness begets kindness. No matter to what degree you contribute, you can make the world a better place.

When you are living a balanced, well-nourished life, you have the best foundation to serve the world through your purpose. Sometimes people can get overzealous and drained working for a cause or following their passions—perhaps this has been you. But you can do it differently now. You can contribute to the world from a well-nourished place. That doesn't mean that you have to wait until some perfect time when all parts of yourself are nourished (as we explored in the multicultural study in chapter 9) to do so, for there is no final destination. Life is dynamic, fluid, and ever changing. Nourishment is a continual unfolding process. It is most helpful and healthful to have your foundational bodies' needs met, but you can be fulfilling others simultaneously.

We will explore ways to connect to your authentic passion and purpose and make a difference in the world in the following Skills and Tools section. You may find your worldly body is interrelated with how you are nourishing your other bodies. Have fun engaging the worldly body and creating the weave of your life. You are in charge. As you continue to put attention on the areas most important to you now, you decide when you are ready to take action and what you want to focus on. You can pause and listen to your inner wisdom centers.

Let's look at how fulfilled and engaged your worldly body is currently in your life and how connected you are to your sense of purpose.

AWARENESS

○ Pause ○ Reflect ○ Assess

How true are the following statements?

~ *I feel a clear sense of meaning and purpose in my life, which I actively engage.*

~ *I contribute to the world in ways that are fulfilling and connected to my sense of purpose.*

~ *I contribute to a cause, volunteer, or have work that is linked to making the world a better place.*

~ *I feel passionate about making a difference in the world.*

~ *I am doing what I love.*

~ *I am aware of my unique gifts.*

If you answered no to any of these questions, you may greatly benefit by nourishing your worldly body.

Mindful Check-In

What do I notice in my mind, body, heart, and spirit when I feel connected to my sense of purpose? How often do I engage in activities that support this? What are they? What helps me feel connected? How does this kind of nourishment feed me? Does it take the focus off food when I'm not physically hungry? Do I ever eat mindlessly when I am making meaningful contributions? If so, what is out of balance? What other body may need attention and care? How do I best stay in balance?

INTENTION

Create an intention(s) based on your inquiry and reflection around nourishment of the worldly body. Do you want to bring greater awareness to this part of your life? Is it a time in your life when you want to do more soul searching and align yourself more with purposeful living? Do you want to develop more opportunities to contribute, or to have practices in your life to nourish the worldly body? Do you want to find what you are passionate about? Write your intention below and/or in your Well Nourished Journal.

_____

_____

_____

_____

SKILLS AND TOOLS

You are likely reading this chapter because you want to embody your unique purpose and contribution more fully, or because you want to find out what it is in the first place. Your sense of purpose can change over a lifetime, necessitating a deeper look or creating a new venture for your gifts to be received.

Finding your purpose is a process of mindful inquiry and exploration seasoned with grace. Embodying it fully can be a process of both inner unfolding and building an outer structure and support. We'll explore both these facets of authentically living the worldly body.

Find Your Purpose

1. Take a few mindful breaths. Follow the breath with your attention. Wait for the mind to become just a little quieter.
2. Take out your Well Nourished Journal. Make a five-column chart. As you write, let your words flow freely. Don't edit yourself. Let your passionate responses and more shy responses flow. You'll find some columns will be more full than others.

~ *In column 1 write down everything you really love to do in your life.*

~ *In column 2 write down what is most meaningful to you in your life: your deepest values, your passions. If you had one message to share with others, what would it be?*

~ *In column 3 write down the most meaningful ways you love to serve, to help others, now and in the future. What is most fulfilling? What are you passionate about?*

~ *In column 4 write down all your unique gifts (some of those may already be included in columns 1 to 3). What do you love to do and what are you good at? What qualities or abilities do you receive positive feedback on?*

~ *In column 5 write down the difference you would like to see in the world. What causes, people, animals, environments do you feel passionate about?*

1 What I really love to do:	2 What is most meaningful, my deepest values, my one message:	3 How I love to serve and help:	4 My unique gifts are:	5 How I would like to see a difference in the world:

3. Look at column 3. Does a personal mission statement emerge for you? What inspires you and what do you feel passionate about?

Inspiring Statement:

_____

_____

4. Look at all the columns and connect the commonalities with a highlighter. Where is there the most overlap? How do what you love to do, your gifts, how you like to serve, and the difference you most would like to see in the world match up? If they don't, is there a way you can connect the dots?

You may have more than one connecting line running through each of the columns. Perhaps you can see a new way to engage your gifts and contribute to the world. Maybe these disparate things have come together in a way that is exciting and inspiring for you.

Engage Your Wisdom and Grace

Finding your purpose is not a rational process, but writing out your responses in the exercise above can help set the stage. Pause and reflect on these lists and the different connections you have made. Meditate on them. Bring them to mind when you are in nature or in the shower! Let your mind go to these when you first wake up. It's those moments when the linear mind is quiet and the holistic mind is engaged that new connections and insight can best occur. A sense of purpose is given like a gift. One moment it is suddenly there and fills you like a warm flame or blooming flower.

Proclaim Your Sense of Purpose

Pause and take a few mindful breaths. Write out your sense of purpose here and/or in your Well Nourished Journal. If you're still not sure, write what you feel most inspired about currently

_____

_____

_____

Next see if you can connect your sense of purpose to your original and overall intention in one statement. For example:

Overall Intention: *to be healthy and vibrant*
Your Purpose (to make a difference in the world): *to help the world become a healthier, more loving, kind, and peaceful place*

Embody Your Purpose and Unique Contribution

How does your sense of purpose relate to what you are already doing through your worldly body? Is your engagement with the arts, intellectual pursuits, social justice, education connected to what you feel very passionate about; is it contributory in some way? Have you put engaging your sense of purpose on the back burner of a busy life? Do you ever stuff yourself with food to fill that void?

If you are not currently engaged in activities that feel purposeful and meaningful to you, look at the columns from the Find Your Purpose exercise. Play with a way you can combine your gifts and talents with serving a cause or passion in column 4 that you care deeply about that will make a difference—maybe volunteering in your local animal shelter or offering your talents (lessons of any kind, entertainment, music, food preparation, support groups) to homeless women and children in a temporary shelter. If you're great at organizing, what is a need in your community that you care deeply about? If you are not satisfied, try another way of serving and offering your unique gifts and talents. Maybe use the Internet to broaden your scope and make a difference on a larger scale. The rewards and gratitude from service, and especially service that is connected to a sense of purpose, that flows to you is a very different kind of sustenance.

Use Your Gifts

List three new ways you can use your gifts and talents to make a difference. Think about the people, the groups, that would most benefit. Write out these ideas below and/or in your Well Nourished Journal and make a plan to try them out.

1. _____

2. _____

3. _____

Connect Your Intention–Purpose–Unique Contribution

Take your intention and purpose statement from above and connect them to a contribution. You may have many ways to manifest your purpose in your life, from those close around you to a larger societal or planetary level. Choose a few and put them into affirming action statements below. You might find one facet of your broader purpose and make it more specific here. For example:

Overall Intention: *to be healthy and vibrant*
Your Purpose*: to teach others self-kindness and compassion*
Your Unique Contribution: *teaching mindfulness in the schools and volunteering*

_____

_____

_____

_____

Now strengthen your purpose statement. Is it inspiring and energizing to you? If you notice any hesitation, check into any beliefs, thoughts, or feelings that might be holding you back from fully embodying it. Practice letting go of these blocks with skills from chapter 6. Challenge them or use the ALLOWS process (see page 104). Notice what skills, tools, and support you may need to actually manifest your purpose statement. Further training? Joining organizations, teaming up with others? Attending mindfulness retreats or trainings? When you create your SPRIGS goals at the end of this chapter, ask yourself what you need to manifest your purpose or support it further.

Here are just a few examples of ways others have put together their gifts with what they love doing and feel passionate about, the way they like to serve and make a difference in an area they care deeply about.

Cecilia: After years of struggling with weight and body image, never feeling like enough, Cecilia found peace with food and herself through mindful eating and living and making choices to nourish her whole self. She decided to give back to the community in an area very near and dear to her heart. She was a teacher, with a gift to inspire. She loved to educate. She felt passionate about teaching young women tools for self-acceptance and self-love to overcome the influence of distorted body shape and sizes in the media, and mindful eating and healthy lifestyle practices. She chose high schools as her population and young career women in the Big City. She volunteered, then worked in a program and began to develop her own program matching her bigger vision.

Laney: Laney grew up in the mountains, enjoying the seasons, the beauty, and the freedom that access to the acres of parkland offered her, her friends, and her family. When she moved to the city after college, she became acutely aware of how many of her contemporaries weren't comfortable spending time in nature and chose electronics or movies over a hike or picnic. She also saw how some of them snacked incessantly at work or used food to feel better after a stressful day. She created a business offering yoga hikes, bringing people out into nature during lunch breaks and on the weekends. She donated a portion of the modest income to local land trusts that bought up land for parks and protection in perpetuity.

Jennifer: As Jennifer healed from her obsession with food (always thinking about the next meal, what and how much she should eat, often overeating), through mindful eating and living practices, she found she enjoyed cooking for her clients more. She felt in control by eating regularly, honoring what her body really needed, and savoring the food she did eat. She felt a deeper sense of fulfillment and satisfaction from rounding out her life with more activities when she wasn't working as a cook. She was able to recommit to her profession with more zest, zeal, and passion. She really loved and was passionate about preparing and sharing good, healthy food and her knowledge with her clients for their own healing. She no longer needed to worry about her own overeating, being around food so much.

Making a Worldly Difference

Every time you practice lovingkindness meditation and extend the wish that all living beings be happy, peaceful, and at ease, you are contributing to more peace, compassion, and love in yourself and to the world. Every time you stop the struggle inside yourself with mindful practices, you create more peace in yourself and with your interactions with others. Every time you transform a challenging emotion, that's potentially one less harsh word to another or one less cream puff that you didn't really need. Energy is freed up to contribute to the world in a variety of kind ways.

Awareness of your interconnection can impact your own relationship to food. When hunger arises for food when you are not physically hungry, you can think about the ways you are making a difference today, yesterday, in the future. You can mindfully come back to the moment and feel your interconnection with all life. You can enjoy eating a meal or any snack contemplating the awareness of interconnectedness. This may affect your choices, making them more sustainable in the future, as you become more discerning about where you buy your food, considering how it was grown and what kind of impact it has on the environment. All these simple acts can make a difference in the planet we share.

Your SPRIGS Goals

Take out your Well Nourished Journal. Make any SPRIGS goals to help put your intention–purpose–contribution statement into action. What do you need to be, practice, learn, do to put this into action?

_____

_____

_____

_____

OUTER SUPPORT

Create the support in your life you need for your soul's offering. How can you make rewarding and satisfying contributions connected to a sense of purpose and your values? Do you need to do research to learn more about a specific area in which you'd like to offer your skills or organizational or teaching abilities? Would you like to put a team together or create a group to go out and volunteer? Who is already in your social network or what activities could help? Check in with your check-in buddy; perhaps you can work together. Would you like to improve your public speaking or writing skills? Or learn about fund-raising? Make a plan and put it into bite-size action steps. Map what you need to do, where, and when over the time period you choose. Spend time in a way that inspires and supports your vision.

INNER RESOURCES

When you feel the urge to eat, take a Mindful Check-In. Am I physically hungry? Is this a meal or snack time? What do I really need right now? Have I fed my worldly body today by contributing? Am I living this day connected to my values and sense of purpose? This week? Am I making action steps and decisions connected to my values? What do I need to plan for now or later today that would help support nourishment of my worldly body? Plan your day so you have ample opportunities for mindful pausing, gratitude, and appreciation of the moment.

Use Your 5 Steps Prompter Tools

[ ] Fill in the worldly body in your Well Nourished Bowl.

[ ] Fill out your Intention and Goals Prompter for the worldly body.

[ ] Use your 5 Steps Daily Prompter to help support you in mindful choices.

CHAPTER TWELVE

A Plan for the Well-Nourished Life

A well-nourished life is remembering to make the choices that move you toward connection, community, love, well-being, compassion, kindness, and equanimity—choices that help you love, appreciate, and enjoy your life and those around you. Choices that remind you to be kind to yourself and to others.

We have gone on a journey together, exploring what you really need to feel satisfied and nourished in your life way beyond food. You've been encouraged to listen to your whole-body wisdom, to make informed, discerning choices that give you true nourishment to lead a balanced, happy, fulfilled life. You have learned how to use inner resources to nourish your heart, mind, body, and spirit as well as outer tools to create a life and circumstances to support a fuller expression of you. You've learned how to nourish all the bodies that are part of your wholeness through mindfully checking in, using your tools and skills, and perhaps most important, giving yourself permission to do so. If you still have any lingering doubts, remember that this is not a selfish focus. Happier, more fulfilled people are actually more apt to help others, contribute to society and the world, and spread the happiness with smiles and acts of kindness, compassion, and thoughtfulness. You are worth it—for yourself, everyone you care about, and the world.

You've learned guidelines for eating without guilt or shame and making choices that are enjoyable, delicious, healthful, and pleasurable to you—a way to actually enjoy your food more, to truly savor it while being able to eat less in quantity. Following the approach in this book, you can actually begin to get your life back from any tyranny of obsession with food.

Life is dynamic. We think we have our plans all figured out, and then some outer or inner circumstance changes. This chapter explores how to bring together a supportive, sustainable plan that is adaptable as you evolve and life changes. What is really nourishing to you now may not be the same as in six months, or a year, or even a few days. Staying mindful and present in the midst of it all is key. We'll build upon several concrete planning tools that can make it easier.

Pause and Reflect

Pause and take a few moments to reflect on any changes you have made since you picked up this book. Perhaps you have just been casually reading through the book. Or you may be actively using the steps in each chapter to implement changes in your life to nourish each of your bodies. Over time these begin to add up, and when you look back over the life you were living before, it might look blander, with little seasoning, than the life you are living now. The life you choose can be rich with delectable new ingredients and garnishes that tickle your soul, inspire your mind, open your heart, and renew your body. Ask yourself:

Have I noticed any decreases in:

~ *The amount of time spent on challenging or distressing thoughts or feelings about food, eating, or body image?*
~ *Overeating or restricting behaviors with food?*
~ *Other behaviors (overworking, isolating, procrastinating) that I have used to soothe, numb, or distract from emotional discomfort?*

Have I noticed any increases in:
~ *Time spent simply being able to enjoy food for the sake of nourishment and pleasure?*
~ *Being more aware of hunger, fullness, and other satiety signals?*
~ *Honoring and respecting my body through the choices I make?*
~ *Eating to satisfaction without becoming overfull?*
~ *Choosing more nutritious food?*
~ *Taking more time to plan, shop, and eat meals mindfully?*

~ More nourishing activities, both inner and outer, for the physical, emotional, psychological, social, intellectual, creative, spiritual, and worldly bodies?

What practices have I begun to incorporate into my life for inner nourishment?

~ Mindful Check-In	~ Appreciation
~ Mindful eating core skills	~ Savoring the good
~ Regular sitting meditation	~ Thought breather
~ Mindfulness of the moment's activity	~ Labeling
~ Mindfulness of breath	~ ALLOWS
~ Spacious mind practice	~ Positive intentions
~ Lovingkindness	~ Affirmations
~ Self-compassion	~ Passion-purpose
~ General compassion	~ Service/my contributions
~ Gratitude	_____ (other)

What healthy lifestyle practices have I begun to incorporate for outer nourishment? What physically nourishing activities am I doing that support all the bodies?

For Physical Nourishment

~ Mindful eating practices

~ Healthy nutrition

~ Exercise

~ Movement

~ Sleep

~ Relaxation

Nourishing Activities for My Other Bodies

~ *Overall nourishing activity list*

~ *Emotional and psychological nourishment activities*

~ *Social and community building*

~ *Intellectual activities*

~ *Creative activities*

~ *Creative living/thinking*

~ *Soul-nourishing activities*

~ *Spiritual activities*

~ *Worldly activities: connected to purpose and passion*

Assess: Gauge and Reenergize Your Journey

Take out your Well Nourished Journal and write for five to seven minutes, without editing, any changes in your life, any shifts that you have noticed since you first began this book. Include what, if anything, has changed regarding the amount of time you focus on eating and food in your life. The following questions might prompt you:

~ *What areas of your life have increased in nourishment?*

~ *What new possibilities have opened up for you?*

~ *Do you have any new eating behaviors? New ways to provide inner and outer nourishment to yourself?*

~ *How do you feel about your mindfulness practices?*

~ *Are there any you want to recommit to?*

~ *Do you want to increase the time you practice in sitting meditation or other foundational mindfulness practices, commit to eating another meal or snack a day mindfully, or try any of the other practices?*

Your Planning Tools

Let's look at the Well Nourished planning tools that you can use to stay on track—to support any changes you have made and to meet life with fresh and wise mindful choices in each moment. Some of these you have been using, some of these are new and will bring everything together.

1. ***Your Well Nourished Bowl:*** a bowl filled with ingredients of your life (skills, activities, practices, people) that nourish you. This is for inspiration, a reminder, and a guide.

2. ***Your Intention and Goals Prompter:*** A quick worksheet of the 5 steps for each body: your intention, the skills and tools (your specific ingredients) to support it, your SPRIGS goals, and the kinds of resources you are calling upon to support each of your bodies. It helps you stay on track to nourishing each part of yourself.

3. ***Your Daily Prompter:*** a nice summary guide to help you make mindful choices in the moment throughout the day.

Fill Your Bowl

Let's take a look at your Well Nourished Bowl, which you have been filling as you've gone through the chapters. Let's also review your intention and goal prompt sheets for each body. Are these up to date, do you want to revise them—are there any new intentions, goals, activities, or skills you can now add to the bowl? Any you would like to add for the future (perhaps put these in a different color)? At this point, you can write down your overall intention and your sense of purpose in the center circle—to continue to inform and inspire what you add to your bowl. You can use your purpose statement if you'd like. It may be that you now need to start a new bowl, as the reality of your life has shifted with your new skills and tools. If you'd like, you can get creative and fill in the sections with color, drawings, or collage to represent each part of yourself now, in addition to words. For some, a Well Nourished Bowl will actually be a little emptier, have a sense of spaciousness, leaving time for contemplation, being-ness, rest, leisure, and mindfulness.

Post your Well Nourished Bowl on your wall or carry it with you as a reminder and for inspiration. You can put those ingredients right into your calendar for daily, weekly, and monthly activities. Use the support of your Intention Prompter Sheet with the 5 steps.

Inspire Your Future

You can also make a new bowl to inspire your future. Fill out a second bowl that represents where you would like to be in three months or one year. Use it as a guidepost and reminder to set your course in your current bowl.

Remember to keep your bowl up to date. Sometimes activities that have been nourishing to us stop being so for various reasons, even with the best of intentions and plans. If we are tuned in mindfully, we can notice this, move out of the automatic habit, and replace it with new practices that are true to this period in our lives. Readjust your bowl, add to it, or make new ones as often you need to—weekly, monthly, biannually. Life isn't linear, so be sure to leave room to fill your bowl with plenty of the mystery, magic, and spontaneity that life brings. This exercise is meant to be ongoing. Visit my website to receive a copy you can download and update as much as you like. Have fun with this and be creative!

Use Your Intention and Goals Prompter

Regularly revisit the intention(s) you have made for each body, the skills and tools that resonate with you and your SPRIGS goals. Update your SPRIGS goals if needed by "upleveling" or adding new activities or skills. When you have satisfactorily integrated the goal into your life, you will always reassess and adjust as you like. Remember, these prompts are meant to be helpful and supportive in staying mindful. You may find that you no longer need to use them at some point, or may just refer to them, review them, and update occasionally.

Well Nourished Daily Prompter

Refer to the Daily Prompter sheet during the day to help you stay mindful in the moment. After a while you likely will not need it, as mindfully checking in will become a new positive habit. It may be especially helpful during times of transition, emotional stress, challenges, or traveling.

Mindful Check-In:

~ *Am I physically hungry?*

~ *What do I really need?*

~ *What is my true need in this moment?*

~ *Can I give that to myself right now?*

~ *What is the nourishing choice?*

Your Mindful Eating Picnic Box

You can neatly pack up and bring with you the mindful eating skill set you have learned, wherever you are, any time. With regular practice, remembering to engage, and being kind and gentle with yourself (when you forget, are on automatic pilot, or "mess up") you can stay on your path.

Bring it with you wherever you are, and consciously engage or not. You can practice eating with the same pleasure, enjoyment, and attention as if you were picnicking in the wine country on a grassy knoll in the spring sunshine. You are hearing the pleasing notes of your favorite music rising and falling in the light breeze, sipping wine, and enjoying locally grown, sustainable, delicious food. Remember, healthy eating can include treats in moderation. Savoring makes less so much more.

At first we eat slowly when we practice mindful eating. The slow pace can be likened to the training wheels we use to learn to ride a bike. As we become more practiced and hone our attention skills, mindful eating becomes more natural. We learn to eat mindfully not only slowly but at different paces (sometimes schedules and life necessitate this), settings, alone and with others. Ideally, we have learned to slow down and really enjoy and be present with food at a pace we can bring with us into all our life situations.

Maintain and Enrich Your Changes

Mindful attention and your new tools are especially helpful in times of stress. Getting back on track is always only one breath away, and that breath becomes now, the only moment you ever truly have to live in, fully inhabit, and make positive choices for yourself, your community, and the planet. Use your tools of Inner Resources and Outer

Support to help you stay on track. If you slip a little, if your bowl spills a little, fill it back up again. Nourishment is only one practice, one action or activity, one hug away.

If there are times in your life when your bowl feels empty, your container of mindfulness, kind awareness, and all the positive qualities you can tap into with practice, essentially your true nature, are always there. As long as you touch into this knowing, you are always whole, never empty (or as Buddhists might say, "Are we not ultimately empty?").

Living a well-nourished life is remembering to make the choices that move you toward connection, community, love, safety, well-being, compassion, kindness, and equanimity—choices that help you love, appreciate, and enjoy your life and those around you. Choices that remind you to be kind to yourself and forgiving. Choices that balance activity with rest, relaxation, and inspiration, incorporating mindful practices that help you stay present for your life. With your bowl full of both inner and outer nourishment, the focus can finally be off food as your main source of pleasure or comfort. When you do eat, you can truly savor your food, enjoy making conscious choices, and relish the healthy eating that makes you feel good and supports your whole, well-nourished life.

Bon appétit!

References

Alberts, H. J., **S. Mulkens**, **M. Smeets**, and **R. Thewissen**. (August 2010). Coping with food cravings. *Appetite*, 55(1), 160–63.

Albertson, **Ellen R.**, **Kristin D. Neff**, and **Karen E. Dill-Shackleford**. (2014). Self-compassion and body dissatisfaction in women: A randomized controlled trial of a brief meditation intervention. *Mindfulness*, 1-11, doi: 10.1007/s12671-014-0277-3.

Baas, **M.**, **C. K. De Dreu**, and **B. A. Nijstad**. A meta-analysis of 25 years of mood-creativity research: Hedonic tone, activation, or regulatory focus? (November 2008). *Psychological Bulletin*, 134(6), 779–806.

Campbell, **T. Colin**, and **Thomas M. Campbell**. (January 2005). *The China Study*. Dallas, TX: BenBella Books.

Cao, **Weifang**, **Xinyi Cao**, **Changyue Hou**, et al. (2016). Effects of cognitive training on resting-state functional connectivity of default mode, salience, and central executive networks. *Frontiers in Aging Neuroscience*, 8, 70.

Chiesa, **Alberto**, and **Alessandro Serretti**. (May 2009). Mindfulness-based stress reduction for stress management in healthy people: A review and meta-analysis. *Journal of Alternative and Complementary Medicine*, 15(5), 593–600.

Epel, **Elissa S.**, **Elizabeth H. Blackburn**, and **Jue Lin**. (2004). Accelerated telomere shortening in response to life stress. *Proceedings of the National Academy of Sciences of the United States of America*, 101(49).

Epstein, **Robert**, **Steven M. Schmidt**, and **Regina Warfel**. (2008). Measuring and training creativity competencies: Validation of a new test. *Creativity Research Journal*, 20(1).

Epton, **T.**, and **P. R. Harris**. (November 2008). Self-affirmation promotes health behavior change. *Health Psychology*, 27(6), 746–52.

Grossman, **P.**, **L. Niemann**, **S. Schmidt**, and **H. Walach**. (July 2004). Mindfulness-based stress reduction and health benefits: A meta-analysis. *Journal of Psychosomatic Research*, 57(1), 35–43.

Kang, **J. H.**, **A. Ascherio**, and **F. Grodstein**. (May 2005). Fruit and vegetable consumption and cognitive decline in aging women. *Annals of Neurology*, 57(5), 713–20.

Keng, **Shian-Ling**, **Moria J. Smoski**, and **Clive J. Robins**. (August 2011). Effects of mindfulness on psychological health: A review of empirical studies. *Clinical Psychology Review*, 31(6), 1041–56.

Kim-Prieto, **Chu**. *Religion and Spirituality across Cultures* (Springer Science + Business Media, 2014): 205–9.

Kristeller, **Jean**, **Ruth Q. Wolever**, and **Virgil Sheets**. (2012). Mindfulness-based eating awareness training (MB-EAT) for binge eating: A randomized clinical trial. *Mindfulness*, 3(4), doi: 10.1007/s12671-012-0179-1.

Leproult, **R.**, **G. Copinschi**, **O. Buxton**, and **E. Van Cauter**. (October 1997). Sleep loss results in an elevation of cortisol levels the next evening. *Sleep*, 20(10), 865–70.

Marmot, **M. G.**, and **S. L. Syme**. (September 1976). Acculturation and coronary heart disease in Japanese-Americans. *American Journal of Epidemiology*, 104(3), 225–47.

Mason, A. E., **E. S. Epel**, **K. Aschbacher**, **R. H. Lustig**, **M. Acree**, **J. Kristeller**, et al. (May 1, 2016). Reduced reward-driven eating accounts for the impact of a mindfulness-based diet and exercise intervention on weight loss: Data from the SHINE randomized controlled trial. *Appetite*, 100, 86–93.

Matsui, T., **T. Ishikawa**, **H. Ito**, **M.**, et al. (February 1, 2012). Brain glycogen supercompensation following exhaustive exercise. *Journal of Physiology*, 590(3): 607–16.

O'Reilly, Gillian A., **Lauren Cook**, **Donna Spruijt-Metz**, and **David S. Black.** (June 2014). Mindfulness-based interventions for obesity-related eating behaviors: A literature review. *Obesity Review*, 15(6), 453–61. doi: 10.1111/obr.12156. Epub March 18, 2014.

Parisi, Jeanine M., **George W. Rebok**, **Qian-Li Xue**, et al. (2012). The role of education and intellectual activity on cognition. *Journal of Aging Research*, 2012, article ID 41613.

Piff, P. K., **P. Dietze**, and **M. Feinberg.** (June 2015). Awe, the small self, and prosocial behavior. *Journal of Personality and Social Psychology*, 108(6), 883–99.

Puchalski, Christina M. (October 2001). The role of spirituality in health care. *BUMC Proceedings*, 14(4), 352–57.

Silvia, Paul J., **Roger E. Beaty**, **Emily C. Nusbaum**, et al. (May 2014). Everyday creativity in daily life: An experience-sampling study of 'little c' creativity. *Psychology of Aesthetics, Creativity, and the Arts*, 8(2), 183–88.

Stellar, Jennifer E., **Neha John-Henderson**, **Craig L. Anderson**, et al. (April 2015). Positive affect and markers of inflammation: Discrete positive emotions predict lower levels of inflammatory cytokines. *Emotion*, 15(2), 129–33.

Stuckey, Heather L., and **Jeremy Nobel.** (February 2010). The connection between art, healing, and public health: A review of current literature. *American Journal of Public Health*, 100(2), 254–63.

Sun, J., **Q. Chen**, and **Q Zhang**, et al. (May 9, 2016). Training your brain to be more creative: Brain functional and structural changes induced by divergent thinking training. *Human Brain Mapping,* doi: 10.1002/hbm.23246. [Epub ahead of print].

Tay, Louis, and **Ed Diener.** (August 2011). Needs and subjective well-being around the world. *Journal of Personality and Social Psychology*, 101(2), 354–65.

Tuso, Philip J., **Mohamed H. Ismail**, **Benjamin P. Ha**, and **Carole Bartolotto**. (Spring 2013). Nutritional update for physicians: Plant based diets. *Permanente Journal*, 17(2), 61–66.

Tyrväinen, Liisa Ann Ojala, **Kalevi Korpela**, et al. (June 2014). The influence of urban green environments on stress relief measures: A field experiment. Journal of Environmental Psychology, 38, 1–9.

Ulrich, Roger S. (April 27, 1984). View through a window may influence recovery from surgery. *Science*, 224(4647), 420–21.

Umberson, Debra, and **Jennifer Karas Montez**. (2010). Social relationships and health: A flashpoint for health policy. *Journal of Health and Social Behavior*, 51(Suppl), S54–S66.

Wansink, Brian, and **Jeffery Sobal**. (January 2007). Mindless eating: The 200 daily food decisions we overlook. *Environment and Behavior*, 39(1), 106–23.

Acknowledgments

This book was really birthed over many years, with appreciation and thanks to all the wonderful people who have enriched and inspired my career and life. A big appreciation to senior editor Jill Alexander, editor at Fair Winds Press, and to my editor, Julia Gavria, both of whom helped steward this book with their thoughtfulness and skill and to everyone at Fair Winds Press, including Marissa Giambrone and John Gettings, for supporting this vision to fruition. Many thanks to David Sobel and Steven Freedman, who opened doors to me to help bring Mindfulness and Mind Body Spirit programs to Kaiser Permanente Northern California, and to all my dedicated colleagues there. A special thank you to Jon Kabat-Zinn, founder of MBSR, who started me on the most rewarding path of teaching Mindfulness in 1993. And great gratitude to Elissa Epel, pioneering researcher and professor at UCSF, who introduced me to Jean Kristeller, founder of MB-EAT, and the UCSF team, who showed me the inspiring ways nutrition, eating, and mindfulness can be brought together in evidence-based programs. A special appreciation to Jean for inviting me to join her in facilitating MB-EAT mindful eating professional trainings. I'm also grateful for Chris Germer and Kristin Neff, who are bringing the science of Mindful Self-Compassion to the world. In great gratitude to all the senior guiding teachers at Spirit Rock Meditation Center and Insight Meditation Society, whom I've learned from and sat retreats with over the years and to Anam Thubten for his teachings. Appreciation to my teachers and colleagues Rick Hanson, Linda Graham, James Baraz, Jane Baraz, Bob Stahl, Joanna Macy, and so many others. I'm deeply grateful to my supportive community of friends and colleagues during this book process: Ariana Candell, Carol and Paul Benson, Laura Biron, Ruth and Bruce Davis, Jill Lublin and Steve Lillo, Cindy Stack-Keer, Christine Tulis, Anodea Judith, Barbara Kaplan, Vicki Rae, Jai Josefs, Kathleen Mulligan; and those that offered support in the initial stages of this book-writing process: Marci Shimoff, Byron Belitsos, Francesca Minerva, and Randy Peyser. Huge appreciation to my beloved family, my parents, David and Lois Epel, who instilled wonderful values, love, and opportunities, always offering their caring and insightful counsel; and to my inspiring and wise sisters Sharon Epel and Elissa Epel, who offered invaluable feedback for this book. Lastly, this book wouldn't have been possible without the love, patience, support, and understanding of my husband David and my son Joshua. David was an amazing help throughout, for which I am forever grateful.

About the Author

Andrea Lieberstein, MPH, RDN, RYT, is a mindfulness-based registered dietitian; mindful eating expert and speaker; mindfulness-based stress reduction and mindful self-compassion instructor; and registered yoga instructor. Andrea has been teaching mindfulness meditation since 1993 and leads mindfulness and mindful eating retreats and trainings at renowned retreat centers such as Esalen Institute, Kripalu Yoga Center, Omega Institute, Spirit Rock Meditation Center, and internationally. She speaks at conferences, universities, and worksites such as Google. As a teacher trainer, she trains health professionals in mindfulness-based eating awareness training (MB-EAT), other mindfulness practices, maintains a local and virtual private practice, and was a leader in developing and implementing Mindfulness and Mind Body Spirit programs at Kaiser Permanente Northern California for over twenty years. She was also a consultant and instructor in mindful eating research at the UCSF Osher Center for Integrative Medicine.

Andrea utilizes evidence-based mindfulness and mindful eating practices in her integrative private practice, working with individuals on a wide range of disordered eating, nutrition, and lifestyle challenges; healthy weight management; body image and stress-related issues; and health concerns. She is also trained in integrative and functional nutrition approaches.

She is a contributing author to *Resources for Teaching Mindfulness: An International Handbook* and contributed to the books *The Relaxation and Stress Reduction Workbook* and *Some Leaders Are Born Women*. Andrea has degrees from both Stanford University and University of California, Berkeley. One of her greatest joys is bringing the life-transforming practices of mindfulness and mindful eating and living to others, opening the door to the abiding calm, peace, joy, well-being, and clear seeing these practices offer.

For bonus support tools and more information about Andrea, her programs, and other offerings, visit her websites at www.yourwellnourishedlife.com and www.mindfuleatingtraining.com.

Index